Our Evil—God's Good

Other Works by Al Hill

O Come, Let God Adore Us
And Other Sermons for Advent and Christmas

Not Exactly What They Expected
And Other Sermons for Holy Week and Easter

Things That Kings Can't Do
And Other Sermons from Judges through 2ⁿᵈ Kings, and the Wisdom Books

In the Presence of the Lord
And Other Sermons from the Psalms and the Prophets

Walking with Jesus
And Other Sermons from the Gospel of Matthew

God's Purpose for Your Faith
And Other Sermons from the Gospel of Mark, Hebrews, James and 1ˢᵗ Peter

From Jerusalem to Jericho
And Other Sermons from the Gospel of Luke and the Acts of the Apostles

Traits of the Shepherd
And Other Sermons from the Gospel of John, 1ˢᵗ John and Revelation

Making Peace with Your Father
And Other Sermons from Paul's Letters to the Romans and Corinthians

The Empty God
And Other Sermons from the Shorter Letters of Paul

DEAR TRINITY
Letters from a Pastor to His People

Our Evil—God's Good

And Other Sermons
from Genesis through Judges

Al Hill

SOMMERTON
HOUSE

Cover design by the author.
Stock imagery © Alamy.

The cover image of Joseph's reunion in Egypt with his father Jacob is part of a stained-glass window located in St Andrew's Church in Arthingworth, in Northamptonshire, England. The image is used with the kind permission of St. Andrew's Church.

ISBN: 978-1-948773-21-8 (sc)

Library of Congress Control Number: 2018907349

To learn more about or purchase this or other works by Al Hill,

go to www.sommertonhouse.com,

or www.amazon.com/author/alhill.

Dedication

To the many teachers and preachers
who made the Bible and its people come alive for me
over the past four decades and more.

Many of those who had the most profound influence
on my understanding and appreciation of God's Word
represented traditions
and espoused theological perspectives
very different from my own—
and yet,
their scholarship, imagination, insight and eloquence
have left me forever in their debt.

Foremost among these have been
Frederick Buechner,
Walter Brueggemann,
George Buttrick,
Fred Craddock,
Raymond E. Brown,
Elizabeth Achtemeier,
Kenneth E. Bailey,
David Buttrick,
Don Williams
and
C. S. Lewis.

Contents

Sermons

Indices

Preface

Well, here's where it all begins.

Not in the sermons that follow, of course, but in the books of the Bible from which these sermons come—or, at least, about which the sermons talk. Most of these sermons are based on passages from the Book of Genesis, beginning "In the beginning" with Creation and the all-too-brief, and rudely interrupted, sojourn in Paradise. There is wonder and wickedness, desire and disobedience, insolence and violence—and all that before we even get to the patriarchs and the overarching Promise God makes them that will define individuals and families and a nation before we're done with the books these sermons cover.

Genesis through Joshua say so much about who we are and where we've come from that these most ancient of sacred words cannot be ignored. The question of where we will end up will have to wait for later revelation (or Revelation), but even here, you can get a pretty good idea of where and how the journey starts, and what kind of pilgrimage it will be. There is much in these books to shed light on why we and our world are the way we are.

So often, the stories revolve around troubled relationships between God and individuals—individuals connected to God in precarious yet providential ways, but not properly related as God requires. Where God has created heaven and earth and everything in them to the standard of divine perfection, the crown of His Creation seems bent from the beginning (or Beginning) on creating evil in countless different ways.

And so, the human experience becomes one of human evil contending with the goodness of God. Human depravity meets redemptive divinity. As the original Joseph told his guilty brothers: "The very thing you meant for evil, God meant for good."

And that reality should be worth a few sermons to point it out in the confusion of our contemporary existence.

సాంగ

The sermons in this collection were written as full manuscripts—for the purpose of oral presentation. They were preached to Navy chapel and civilian church congregations over a number of years. In some cases, you will see that passages did "double duty," supporting several sermons. Following the Revised Common Lectionary for some of the years of my preaching ministry led me inevitably back to the same scripture. I assure you that I never exhausted the meaning or inspiration of a passage after only one attempt.

Where it seemed necessary, I have explained something of the context of a sermon: where it was preached or under what special circumstance. Generally, these are sermons you might hear in your church on any Sunday. In fact, all the footnotes within the sermons were added "after the fact" for your convenience. I hope you find them useful. Where I have actually quoted a phrase or verse from a particular version of the Bible, that version is noted along with the reference. Where I paraphrased or merely alluded to something biblical, the reference is provided without a version attached.

Believing you would find it helpful, I have included the biblical text before or within each sermon. The exception to this practice involved those cases when the extreme length of the passage made it impossible (e. g., "The Secret of Survival" on page 121). A few of the sermons were based, originally, on the 1984 edition of the New International Version of the Bible. That edition is no longer available for publication, unfortunately, and so I have, in those few cases, substituted the English Standard Version.

You will note that I capitalize pronouns and other references to Father, Son or Holy Spirit, contrary to the contemporary grammatical convention. I do so as an expression of reverence. Practically, it also tends to provide clarity for the reader when pronouns may refer to any of several individuals. Because there always seems to be an exception, the exception in this instance is in the rendering of copyrighted text: I have left the words from the various versions of the Bible as I found them.

And at the end of the book, you will find several indices. I would have liked to have had lists like these in many of the wonderful books that I used frequently over the years as I sought a wiser pastor's help in getting to the point of what I intended to preach. Perhaps the facility they provide will make up for anything lacking in the sermons themselves.

దుం

Although several volumes of sermons preceded this one, *Our Evil—God's Good* will naturally function as the first in a series that numbers 11 in all. Two of the other books contain additional sermons from the Old Testament; four of the book are devoted to sermons based on each of the Gospels (and related books from the General Epistles, Acts and Revelation), and Paul's Epistles form the basis for the sermons in the last two books. Volumes dealing with Advent and Christmas, and Holy Week and Easter, respectively, have already been published.

దుం

This, and the other books in this series. are being provided, first of all, for colleagues in the ministry of preaching, to help stimulate thought and provide encouragement in the hard work of preparing to stand before God's people and speak His word to them. In addition, I hope that anyone who cares about growing deeper in faith and closer to God will find these words helpful as inspiration or instruction.

Some sacred and familiar words may be appropriate in concluding this preface:

"Glory be to the Father
and to the Son
and to the Holy Ghost;
as it was in the beginning,
is now,
and ever shall be,
world without end.
Amen."[1]

❧❦

---

[1] The *Gloria Patri.*

Sermons

From the Book of Genesis

Genesis 1:1-5 ESV

¹ In the beginning, God created the heavens and the earth. ² The earth was without form and void, and darkness was over the face of the deep. And the Spirit of God was hovering over the face of the waters.

³ And God said, "Let there be light," and there was light. ⁴ And God saw that the light was good. And God separated the light from the darkness. ⁵ God called the light Day, and the darkness he called Night. And there was evening and there was morning, the first day.

ॐ⌘

John 1:1-18 ESV

¹ In the beginning was the Word, and the Word was with God, and the Word was God. ² He was in the beginning with God. ³ All things were made through him, and without him was not any thing made that was made. ⁴ In him was life, and the life was the light of men. ⁵ The light shines in the darkness, and the darkness has not overcome it.

⁶ There was a man sent from God, whose name was John. ⁷ He came as a witness, to bear witness about the light, that all might believe through him. ⁸ He was not the light, but came to bear witness about the light.

⁹ The true light, which gives light to everyone, was coming into the world. ¹⁰ He was in the world, and the world was made through him, yet the world did not know him. ¹¹ He came to his own, and his own people did not receive him. ¹² But to all who did receive him, who believed in his name, he gave the right to become children of God, ¹³ who were born, not of blood nor of the will of the flesh nor of the will of man, but of God.

¹⁴ And the Word became flesh and dwelt among us, and we have seen his glory, glory as of the only Son from the Father, full of grace and truth. ¹⁵ (John bore witness about him, and cried out, "This was he of whom I said, 'He who comes after me ranks before me, because he was before me.'") ¹⁶ For from his fullness we have all received, grace upon grace. ¹⁷ For the law was given through Moses; grace and truth came through Jesus Christ. ¹⁸ No one has ever seen God; the only God, who is at the Father's side, he has made him known.

ॐ⌘

1.

In the Beginning—Again

Genesis 1:1-5; John 1:1-18 ESV

At this church, the Word of God is the substance and the stimulation of our sermons. The Bible is the source of our authority to stand here before you and speak. We will not speak—and you should not hear—anything that is not suggested and supported by God's Word.

And so, we begin—as the Bible does: *"In the beginning...."*

The Bible begins by answering the most crucial question in all of human existence: "Is there a God?" The Bible answers the question, "Yes." *"In the beginning, God...."*

Today, of course, many people, highly educated and otherwise, are convinced the answer is "No."

"There is no God," they say. "The concept of God is a myth—a superstition of the ancient past that has no place in our modern, scientific world."

And the arguments they offer champion perceived scientific certainties with eloquent logic, while ridiculing the idea of divine revelation and rejecting the teachings of traditional religion. And they *"live and move and have* [their] *being"*[2] as though there were no

---

[2] Acts 17:28, ESV.

God, with all the consequences—personal and social—temporal and eternal—that come from such convictions.

But just in case they are wrong and the Bible is right, let us see what the Bible says about this God these so-called superstitious simpletons of the ancient past assure us is real.

❧

"In the beginning, God created the heavens and the earth," they say in sacred scripture.

Interestingly, they simply assume God's existence. The first thing they tell us about God is that He did something: *God created.* *"God created the heavens and the earth"* when they did not exist—*"in the beginning."*

To create the heavens and the earth, God must Himself exist, of course—and exist before anything else that came into existence—in the beginning, or after. The Bible begins by telling us that the world and everything in it—including us—and everything in the vast, seemingly endless expanse of space— exist—and exist *only*—because God created them—in the beginning.

Of course, even the modern scientists believe there was a "beginning." All the data they have amassed empirically and theoretically encourage them to postulate a "beginning"—of cosmic proportions and instantaneous effect. But something about being able to send satellites spiraling into deep space makes it ever so hard to believe that there is a God Who created deep space and sent it spiraling back toward us.

❧

What God did—and continues to do (i.e., create)—provides the first indication of Who the God Who exists *is*.

God is Creator. And not just *a* creator—God is *the* Creator. The Bible tells us, on its very first page, something as simple as it is profound: The Creator created Creation. That's what creating *everything* means.

A single Creator creating means that everything created is part of a single set. Creation is not just a bunch of individual, independent "stuff" that accumulated accidentally. All things are part of this *one* thing: Creation—the Creation created by the Creator. It—and we—are connected—by and with the Creator—at the core of our existence.

❧

And what else does the Bible tell us when it tells us God—the Creator—created all Creation?

Certainly, a God Who can create everything in existence—from nothing—is infinitely powerful. In fact, He did not have to "build" everything; He simply *spoke* it all into existence. God said, *"Let there be light"*—let light exist. And light came into being.

And He did that sort of thing over and over again, as long as it took to get everything into existence that He wanted to exist. God merely gave the command and His command was carried out by things that, before He commanded their existence, did not exist at all.

That is *sovereign* power. God has the power to call Creation into being. God the Creator calls—and Creation answers by "being."

❧

Having and exercising the ability to create all things makes all things created the rightful property of the Creator. God created all things to be His. God created *us* to be His.

And that God created all things when nothing could require or force Him to create anything suggests that God had a purpose for Creation. *We* have a purpose—a divinely-appointed purpose.

The Creator created Creation in order to possess it and to have it fulfill His purpose. But lest this suggest that this Creator God is coercive or tyrannical, note that, though He could have forced

Creation into existence, He "invited" it to be, instead. He said, "***Let*** *there be…*" and there was.

And when it "was"—first, light, and then everything else—the Creator determined, and expressed the value of, what He had created: *"God saw that it was good"*—in each particular part—and *"very good"* in all the parts together.[3]

❧⤙

In the Sundays to come, we will learn that God created all things—and us—to be obedient to His sovereign will—to be grateful for His unending grace—and to be faithful to Him in response to His faithfulness to His Creation. What we will discover is not that God does not exist, but that God's Creation has chosen to be disobedient, ungrateful and faithless to its Creator—each attitude or behavior, in itself, a form of denial of the Creator God's existence, sovereignty, purpose, and love.

We will discover that the Creator loves and respects His Creation so much that, even in its consistent state of rebellion, He will not destroy it or abandon it. The Creator will constantly seek to restore His Creation—to re-create it to understand, finally, its intended relationship with the Creator—which is to embrace Him and His purpose for it.

❧⤙

That's what John is talking about when he writes that *"The light shines in the darkness, and the darkness has not overcome it. The true light, which gives light to everyone, was coming into the world."*

God created light with His first spoken word to overcome the darkness in which chaos went unchecked. And then one day, the Creator *became* light to overcome the darkness and chaos into which His beloved Creation had sunk, so that His Creation might

---

[3] Genesis 1:10, 12, 18, 21, 25, 31.

once again live in light as He intended. *"To all who did receive Him, who believed in His Name, He gave the right to become children of God."*

৯-৫

Is there a God?

If your answer is "Yes," yours is a world of light and life with a loving, powerful, purposeful, gracious and faithful Creator.

If your answer is "No," you consign yourself to a world *"without form and void, and darkness"*—whether you are right or wrong.

The Bible says, *"In the beginning, God..."*

What do you say?

৯-৫

Genesis 1:1-5 NRSV

¹ In the beginning when God created the heavens and the earth, ² the earth was a formless void and darkness covered the face of the deep, while a wind from God swept over the face of the waters. ³ Then God said, "Let there be light," and there was light. ⁴ And God saw that the light was good; and God separated the light from the darkness. ⁵ God called the light Day, and the darkness he called Night. And there was evening and there was morning, the first day.

≫•≪

2.

A Good Day's Work

Genesis 1:1-5 NRSV

When something is very familiar—when you recognize it easily—you tend not to look at it closely or examine it carefully.

The beginning of the Bible is very familiar. You don't have to be a renowned Bible scholar to recognize *"In the beginning, God created the heavens and the earth"* (and the words that follow).

But have you ever looked at this passage closely? Have you ever taken some time to really examine what the Bible is saying when it says this?

We have a few minutes before the ushers have to take up the offering. Why don't we take a closer look? Why don't we examine this business of "the beginning and God" a bit more carefully, and see if there is anything here we might have missed before?

∂∽∾

Are you aware, for instance, that these words were written, not just to inspire, but to argue a point with the rest of the world?

"In the beginning, God…" is—knowingly and intentionally—an "in-your-face" argument against every other idea about how the world came to be—and more importantly, what life means even now.

There were many ideas in the ancient world about "how it all began," just as there are in our modern world.

Then as now, the Bible is saying, *"In the beginning, God."* God was "there" at the start of everything. God was the One Who started everything. God started everything *because* He wanted to, and He started everything *the way* He wanted to. *"God created the heavens and the earth."*

☙◦❧

This means that the world is no accident; random chance is not the basic law of the universe. And the world was not a mistake. Certainly, *we* have made mistakes, from the very beginning, but our existence—our creation—was not—and is not—a mistake.

The universe did not just "happen" to be; it came to be because Someone *chose* for it to be, *wanted* it to be, *caused* it to be—that Someone being a God Who was there when the universe and everything else was not.

The Bible is also suggesting here—at the very beginning of the words about the very beginning of the world—that there is a Creator God Who does not make mistakes or cause accidents. And the implication is that this is true not only for the beginning, but for the present and the future as well.

What was true of God's work at the dawn of Creation on a cosmic level is also true right now on the individual life level: God makes no mistakes and causes no accidents with you and me.

☙◦❧

Notice what things were like before God got involved. All there was (except for God) was emptiness—completely dark nothingness. Nothing but nothing—and God.

And then, God made "something."

God spoke out of the darkness because that was all there was until God made—created—spoke into existence—something else, something that had never been before: light. And the monopoly of darkness was over—forever.

Once God called light into existence, there was never again a time when darkness was not subject to the light. God did not choose to eliminate darkness completely, but He did choose to subject it to His will.

This is a God Who is not afraid of the dark, or of anything that prefers the dark. This God prefers light over darkness, for He created light to dispel darkness when darkness was all there was. But He is also a God, according to the Psalmist, to Whom even the darkness will not be dark. To this God, the darkness will shine like the day, *"for darkness is as light"* to Him.[4]

ॐ⊸ॐ

Think about this: That God would do anything in the beginning means that God wanted something other than chaos, emptiness, and darkness. There was no power that could force God to create anything—to change anything. There was no supplicant to ask for a change, whether for pleasure or need. There was God and nothing, and God was not satisfied to leave things as they were. God was not willing to accept what He did not want. He obviously wanted something other than what "was" when all there "was" was nothing.

ॐ⊸ॐ

In other words: This God had a purpose. He had a purpose in creating everything He created. And now, everything He created exists because of, and for, that purpose. The universe exists for God's purpose. *You* exist for God's purpose.

And what is that purpose?

A wild guess might be: life—and life in relationship with this Creator God. When there was neither light nor life, when neither

---

4 Psalm 139:12, NRSV.

was *going* to be—through any other means—God created a place for life (earth—dry land), and then created the means for life to exist (by calling forth light and all that comes from light and requires light to live).

Another hint at the purpose of God is that God began by controlling the chaos and the state of overwhelming darkness and emptiness in which life cannot exist. When God creates, He takes what is empty and without form and wrapped in darkness and fills it and forms it to suit His purpose for it. This is His way, cosmically and personally.

കൈ

If your life is *not "without form and void,"* it is because of what God has done to order and enlighten it, whether you recognize His creative presence of not.

But if your life is chaos—if your heart is empty—if your days are dark and your despair as deep as an ocean, the Bible says there is a God Whose Spirit moves across dark, empty chaos like a mighty wind and speaks light and life into existence.

In the beginning of your chaotic, empty life, God created the world you know and the heavens you can only imagine. In the midst of your darkness, God turned on a light the darkness could not withstand.[5] When there was nothing of worth or value or purpose in your life to hold on to, God changed what was, and would have always been without His intervention, into what could only be with Him—and will be—because of Him—forever.

The Creator God separates out the darkness in your life and gives it a limited place and a simple name that shows He controls it. He creates light and gives it to you as a gift and calls it "day" so that you may see Him and live with Him in the world He called into being according to His purpose.

---

[5] John 1:4-5.

When there was nothing, God was there. When there was order and light, God was there. When the world was filled with all good things and heaven rang with infinite glory, the God Who called it all into existence was there to sustain, to guide, to engage and enjoy His Creation.

And when the crown of His Creation chose to be the only part of His creation to resist His voice and reject His purpose, God was there to *re-create* amid the chaos and emptiness and darkness that was now man-made.[6] And He controlled the chaos and dispelled the darkness and filled the emptiness in human hearts as He had in the primal deep—in the beginning.

৯~৯

Isn't it interesting that the beginning is when God changed nothing into something? Before that, there was nothing—no beginning. After that, there was something—something we trace back to a beginning.

And because of that creative command of God, we know God was the Source, the Agent, the Power, the Beginner of the Beginning.

Today, chaos, emptiness, and darkness have got a lot of people convinced it is the end.

Perhaps it is the beginning, instead. Perhaps it is the beginning in which God begins to create out of that chaos and darkness: order, light and life.

What began in darkness ended in light that very first day. Perhaps that's why the Bible says: *"and there was evening and there was morning—the first day."*

In the same way, the Psalmist sings, *"weeping may linger for a night, but joy comes with the morning."*[7]

---

[6] 2 Corinthians 5:17.
[7] Psalm 30:5, NRSV.

"*In the beginning, God created the heavens and the earth.*"
In the beginning, God said, "*Let there be light.*"
In the beginning, God saw that His Creation was good.
In the beginning, God gave life where there had been none.
True then.
True now.
Please take note.

ॐॐ

Genesis 2:4b through 3:24 ESV

2 *2⁴ ...in the day that the Lord God made the earth and the heavens.*

⁵ When no bush of the field was yet in the land and no small plant of the field had yet sprung up—for the Lord God had not caused it to rain on the land, and there was no man to work the ground, ⁶ and a mist was going up from the land and was watering the whole face of the ground— ⁷ then the Lord God formed the man of dust from the ground and breathed into his nostrils the breath of life, and the man became a living creature. ⁸ And the Lord God planted a garden in Eden, in the east, and there he put the man whom he had formed. ⁹ And out of the ground the Lord God made to spring up every tree that is pleasant to the sight and good for food. The tree of life was in the midst of the garden, and the tree of the knowledge of good and evil.

¹⁰ A river flowed out of Eden to water the garden, and there it divided and became four rivers. ¹¹ The name of the first is the Pishon. It is the one that flowed around the whole land of Havilah, where there is gold. ¹² And the gold of that land is good; bdellium and onyx stone are there. ¹³ The name of the second river is the Gihon. It is the one that flowed around the whole land of Cush. ¹⁴ And the name of the third river is the Tigris, which flows east of Assyria. And the fourth river is the Euphrates.

¹⁵ The Lord God took the man and put him in the garden of Eden to work it and keep it. ¹⁶ And the Lord God commanded the man, saying, "You may surely eat of every tree of the garden, ¹⁷ but of the tree of the knowledge of good and evil you shall not eat, for in the day that you eat of it you shall surely die."

¹⁸ Then the Lord God said, "It is not good that the man should be alone; I will make him a helper fit for him." ¹⁹ Now out of the ground the Lord God had formed every beast of the field and every bird of the heavens and brought them to the man to see what he would call them. And whatever the man called every living creature, that was its name. ²⁰ The man gave names to all livestock and to the birds of the heavens and to every beast of the field. But for Adam there was not found a helper fit for him. ²¹ So the Lord God caused a deep sleep to fall upon the man, and while he slept took one of his ribs and closed up its place with flesh. *²² And the rib that the Lord God had taken from the man he made into a woman and brought her to the man.*

²³ Then the man said,

> *"This at last is bone of my bones*
> *and flesh of my flesh;*
> *she shall be called Woman,*
> *because she was taken out of Man."*

²⁴ Therefore a man shall leave his father and his mother and hold fast to his wife, and they shall become one flesh. ²⁵ And the man and his wife were both naked and were not ashamed.

3 ¹ Now the serpent was more crafty than any other beast of the field that the Lord God had made.

He said to the woman, "Did God actually say, 'You shall not eat of any tree in the garden'?" ² And the woman said to the serpent, "We may eat of the fruit of the trees in the garden, ³ but God said, 'You shall not eat of the fruit of the tree that is in the midst of the garden, neither shall you touch it, lest you die.'" ⁴ But the serpent said to the woman, "You will not surely die. ⁵ For God knows that when you eat of it your eyes will be opened, and you will be like God, knowing good and evil." ⁶ So when the woman saw that the tree was good for food, and that it was a delight to the eyes, and that the tree was to be desired to make one wise, she took of its fruit and ate, and she also gave some to her husband who was with her, and he ate. ⁷ Then the eyes of both were opened, and they knew that they were naked. And they sewed fig leaves together and made themselves loincloths.

⁸ And they heard the sound of the Lord God walking in the garden in the cool of the day, and the man and his wife hid themselves from the presence of the Lord God among the trees of the garden. ⁹ But the Lord God called to the man and said to him, "Where are you?" ¹⁰ And he said, "I heard the sound of you in the garden, and I was afraid, because I was naked, and I hid myself." ¹¹ He said, "Who told you that you were naked? Have you eaten of the tree of which I commanded you not to eat?" ¹² The man said, "The woman whom you gave to be with me, she gave me fruit of the tree, and I ate." ¹³ Then the Lord God said to the woman, "What is this that you have done?"

The woman said, "The serpent deceived me, and I ate."
¹⁴ The Lord God said to the serpent,

> "Because you have done this,
>> cursed are you above all livestock
>>> and above all beasts of the field;
>> on your belly you shall go,
>> and dust you shall eat
>>> all the days of your life.
> ¹⁵ I will put enmity between you and the woman,
>> and between your offspring and her offspring;
>> he shall bruise your head,
>> and you shall bruise his heel."

¹⁶ To the woman he said,

> "I will surely multiply your pain in childbearing;
>> in pain you shall bring forth children.
> Your desire shall be contrary to your husband,
>> but he shall rule over you."

¹⁷ And to Adam he said,

> "Because you have listened to the voice of your wife
>> and have eaten of the tree
>>> of which I commanded you,
>>>> 'You shall not eat of it,'
>> cursed is the ground because of you;
>> in pain you shall eat of it all the days of your life;
>> ¹⁸ thorns and thistles it shall bring forth for you;
>> and you shall eat the plants of the field.
> ¹⁹ By the sweat of your face
> you shall eat bread,
>> till you return to the ground,
> for out of it you were taken;
>> for you are dust,
> and to dust you shall return."

²⁰ *The man called his wife's name Eve, because she was the mother of all living.* ²¹ *And the Lord God made for Adam and for his wife garments of skins and clothed them.*

²² *Then the Lord God said, "Behold, the man has become like one of us in knowing good and evil. Now, lest he reach out his hand and take also of the tree of life and eat, and live forever—"* ²³ *therefore the Lord God sent him out from the garden of Eden to work the ground from which he was taken.* ²⁴ *He drove out the man, and at the east of the garden of Eden he placed the cherubim and a flaming sword that turned every way to guard the way to the tree of life.*

❧•❦

Romans 5:12-19 ESV

[12] *Therefore, just as sin came into the world through one man, and death through sin, and so death spread to all men because all sinned—* [13] *for sin indeed was in the world before the law was given, but sin is not counted where there is no law.* [14] *Yet death reigned from Adam to Moses, even over those whose sinning was not like the transgression of Adam, who was a type of the one who was to come.*

[15] *But the free gift is not like the trespass. For if many died through one man's trespass, much more have the grace of God and the free gift by the grace of that one man Jesus Christ abounded for many.* [16] *And the free gift is not like the result of that one man's sin. For the judgment following one trespass brought condemnation, but the free gift following many trespasses brought justification.* [17] *For if, because of one man's trespass, death reigned through that one man, much more will those who receive the abundance of grace and the free gift of righteousness reign in life through the one man Jesus Christ.*

[18] *Therefore, as one trespass led to condemnation for all men, so one act of righteousness leads to justification and life for all men.* [19] *For as by the one man's disobedience the many were made sinners, so by the one man's obedience the many will be made righteous.*

ॐ✎

3.

What Might Have Been

Genesis 2:4b through 3:24; Romans 5:12-19 ESV

Reading the second and third chapters of Genesis—the story of Adam and Eve in the Garden of Eden—is like watching one of those old movies of a train wreck taking place in slow motion. You see the approaching disaster and you despair for the poor people involved, even if the awful tragedy will be their own fault. You want to warn them. You want to reach out and stop them before it's too late: "Look out! Don't do it! You're going to crash!"

But it's already too late. What you are seeing is history— ancient history. Those trains exploded into each other long before you were born. And Adam and Eve's first and flagrant sin collided with God's solitary command before this first man and first woman on earth even had time to get familiar with the paradise God had provided them.

Every time you read the story, you watch the disaster looming all over again: "Eve, don't listen to that serpent! Adam, don't do it!"

If only you could throttle that sneaky little snake before he gets a word out. If only you could knock that fruit out of Eve's hand before she puts it in her mouth. If only they hadn't disobeyed God in the Garden, you think, what might have been—for them and for the whole world.

But it's too late—centuries and millennia too late—for them and for their children and for the whole human race descended from them. And your heart breaks, because you know that it's too late for you, too.

Adam and Eve caused the first human "train wreck" in God's good Creation, but every one of us has hurtled down that same track in our time, with all the reckless abandon of our first ancestors, and far less excuse: We've had the mountains of mangled lives from all the previous wrecks piled up along the way to warn us of the destruction caused by disobedience to the guidance God has given. And we didn't slow down a bit.

❧

You can imagine a Garden of Eden. You can imagine yourself in it. You can imagine a close loving relationship with a gracious God and the helpful partner God has created for you. You can imagine meaningful, enjoyable work that makes God pleased with you and results in an abundant prosperity that wells up in the Garden and waits for you to claim it. You can imagine a long life of perfect health and perpetual happiness. Paradise.

And that's "what might have been"—but for the sin of Adam and Eve—but for your sin and mine.

Do you ever catch yourself wondering "what might have been"? What might have been for the human race if Adam and Eve hadn't committed that first sin? What might my life have been like if I hadn't committed *my* first sin—and all the ones that followed it? As you reflect on the tragic turning points in your life over that cup of coffee in the morning, or replay some less than honorable episode in your life before you go to sleep at night, do you look back on your choices and actions and think, "If only…"?

If only I hadn't smoked that first cigarette. If only I hadn't gotten in with the wrong crowd. If only I hadn't ignored my parents and wasted my opportunities. If only I had been more patient with my kids or devoted to my spouse. If only I had wanted to obey God from the beginning—and done so—rather than doing all the selfish things I chose to do to please myself—and then regretted doing them, immediately, and ever since.

ॐॐ

Why is it so painful to watch Adam and Eve being placed in the Garden by God only to be driven out of it by that same God?

You see the family resemblance.

It's the story of your life, too. It's the story of "what might have been" for you. If only you could go back and do it over—go back and make the right choice—do the right thing.

But you can't. It doesn't work that way. You can't go back and change your past any more than you can change theirs: Father Adam's and Mother Eve's. The past is done, and you can't undo it.

Sin, once committed, unleashes consequences that crash down on us and others—setting even more sin in motion, for though we do at times learn from our mistakes, we continue to fall prey to other temptations. And all of our sins are, at heart, the same one that started the whole tragic derailment of mankind: We do not obey God because we do not trust God to provide for us in the manner we think we can obtain for ourselves and by ourselves.

Whatever God had in mind for your life, your sin has gotten in the way, and there is nothing you can do to reclaim what might have been.

ॐॐ

But that's not the end of the story.

Human sin did and does destroy what might have been, but the God Who punishes sin also provides for the sinner He has punished. Adam and Eve sin against God. They disobey God and do not trust Him to do right by them. God judges them and allows the consequences of their sin to run their course. He drives them from the paradise He designed for them.

But He delivers them from the Garden, out into the harsh world beyond, having dressed them Himself for the more difficult lives they have brought upon themselves.

Will they die as promised?

Yes, but death is delayed. God desires that even those who have sinned against Him have life.[8] This life will be harder than it would have been—should have been. Prosperity will be possible, but elusive. Health will be subject to danger and disease. Happiness will rest on skimpier foundations. Harmony with earth and neighbor and God will be the exception, not the rule. And still God provides for His Creation, despite its rebellion against Him.

Paradise?

No, not anymore.

But life—blessed, grace-filled life?

Yes, even with its grubby legacy of sin. And life—even the hard, diminished life of the sinner—is still a good thing, because God and only God made life, and all that God makes is good.[9]

≈

But that's still not the end of the story.

The God Who created paradise, and human beings to live in it, does not want their sin to prevent them from living in the paradise He has created. While we can only regret "what might have been," God has control of "what might yet be."

The past is done; our sins are fixed in place. But the future is in God's hands and God has chosen in His love and mercy to alter the trajectory of history that Adam and Eve set in motion. Centuries and millennia after Adam and Eve set the unending chain reaction of human train wrecks in motion, God sent a new Adam to stop the chain reaction in its tracks and "un-wreck" the

---

[8] Matthew 18:14.
[9] Genesis 1:31.

trains—to repair the damage to body and soul and society—and set men and women back on the right track with God.

That's what Paul is talking about. He lays it all out in Romans 5: Jesus Christ is the free Gift—the Grace of God—that gives life, the kind of life Adam and Eve lost when they listened to the serpent and swallowed the lie—and the fruit—that forced their expulsion from the Garden.

In Jesus, God undoes everything Adam did to mess up the human race. But it's easier to understand in 1 Corinthians, where Paul says: *"For as in Adam all die, so in Christ all will be made alive."*[10]

It's like running the film backward. Chaos and destruction give way to order and peace and restoration as the engines move farther and farther away from the point of deadly impact. It looks like a miracle.

The biblical equivalent is exactly that. The new Adam, Jesus Christ, Who is as much a man as the old Adam,[11] and as much God as the God Adam disobeyed in the Garden,[12] has taken Adam's sin and Eve's sin and your sin and my sin upon Himself (*"Who knew no sin"*[13]), and by the power and mercy of God, has rerouted the consequences of His grace up the track of our sins to overcome our sinful nature and propel us, not away from God's paradise, but back toward it.

❧

Over a hundred years ago, an American poet wrote,
"For all sad words
of tongue and pen,
The saddest are these,
'It might have been.'"[14]

---

[10] 1 Corinthians 15:22, NIV.
[11] Hebrews 2:17-18.
[12] Colossians 1:19.
[13] 2 Corinthians 5:21, NIV.
[14] From the poem, "Maud Muller," by John Greenleaf Whittier, 1856.

Two thousand years ago, a Jewish Carpenter on a Roman cross wrote, in His blood, the happiest words every sinner who ever lived could ever hope to hear: "It can yet be."

To a dying thief beside Him—another sin-wrecked son of Adam—Jesus put it this way: *"Today, you will be with Me...in Paradise."*[15]

வை

---

[15] Luke 23:43, NIV.

Genesis 4:1-16 ESV

¹ *Now Adam knew Eve his wife, and she conceived and bore Cain, saying, "I have gotten a man with the help of the Lord." ² And again, she bore his brother Abel. Now Abel was a keeper of sheep, and Cain a worker of the ground. ³ In the course of time Cain brought to the Lord an offering of the fruit of the ground, ⁴ and Abel also brought of the firstborn of his flock and of their fat portions. And the Lord had regard for Abel and his offering, ⁵ but for Cain and his offering he had no regard. So Cain was very angry, and his face fell. ⁶ The Lord said to Cain, "Why are you angry, and why has your face fallen? ⁷ If you do well, will you not be accepted? And if you do not do well, sin is crouching at the door. Its desire is contrary to you, but you must rule over it."*

⁸ *Cain spoke to Abel his brother. And when they were in the field, Cain rose up against his brother Abel and killed him. ⁹ Then the Lord said to Cain, "Where is Abel your brother?" He said, "I do not know; am I my brother's keeper?" ¹⁰ And the Lord said, "What have you done? The voice of your brother's blood is crying to me from the ground. ¹¹ And now you are cursed from the ground, which has opened its mouth to receive your brother's blood from your hand. ¹² When you work the ground, it shall no longer yield to you its strength. You shall be a fugitive and a wanderer on the earth." ¹³ Cain said to the Lord, "My punishment is greater than I can bear. ¹⁴ Behold, you have driven me today away from the ground, and from your face I shall be hidden. I shall be a fugitive and a wanderer on the earth, and whoever finds me will kill me." ¹⁵ Then the Lord said to him, "Not so! If anyone kills Cain, vengeance shall be taken on him sevenfold." And the Lord put a mark on Cain, lest any who found him should attack him. ¹⁶ Then Cain went away from the presence of the Lord and settled in the land of Nod, east of Eden.*

ॐ

Matthew 5:21-24 ESV

[Jesus said:]

²¹ *"You have heard that it was said to those of old, 'You shall not murder; and whoever murders will be liable to judgment.'* ²² *But I say to you that everyone who is angry with his brother will be liable to judgment; whoever insults his brother will be liable to the council; and whoever says, 'You fool!' will be liable to the hell of fire.* ²³ *So if you are offering your gift at the altar and there remember that your brother has something against you,* ²⁴ *leave your gift there before the altar and go. First be reconciled to your brother, and then come and offer your gift."*

ও৵৹৻৶

4.

You and Me and God

Genesis 4:1-16; Matthew 5:21-24 ESV

Last week, we learned that getting cross-threaded with God can cost you some prime real estate—and undercut the length and quality of your life as well. Adam and Eve ate the forbidden fruit, and out of Eden they went—and out of the perfect relationship with God and the Garden they had been created to enjoy.[16]

This week, you get to watch as another relationship goes sour: the relationship between the people God created to enjoy His Creation together. God announced early on, that *"it is not good for man to be alone."*[17] But God wasn't just referring to the need to add the female to the mix to be able to make more humans. God could have made as many of us as He wanted, of either gender, the same way He made the first ones.

God created people not just to be persons—individuals—but to become populations—to live and grow in community with each other—and in covenant together with Him.

But it isn't long after people start being born the biological way that the trouble between them begins. Eve gives birth to a couple of boys, Cain and Abel, and though she is happy to get them, that

---

[16] Genesis 3.
[17] Genesis 2:18, ESV.

happiness will not last forever. Her sons will be different, and that difference will ultimately destroy the lives of both. The Bible says they have different jobs—different ways of life—when they grow up. But the difference that brings the danger isn't their doing. It's God's.

෨⠐ᢙ

Cain, the farmer, and Abel, the shepherd, both want to worship God. Both bring their best offering to Him. If there is anything wrong with either of them in what they're doing or how they're doing it, the Bible says nothing about it.

But God responds differently to these two brothers as they attempt to worship Him. He accepts one offering and rejects the other. Cain is the one rejected, and somehow Cain knows this—senses this. God has not blessed Cain the way He has blessed Abel.

And Cain feels the unfairness of it—as we feel all the unfairness we have experienced in life—and all the frustration of not knowing why things don't work out well for us when we try our hardest and do our best.

Why *him*, and not me?!

And a lot of times, we just don't know—and we're not going to know—in this life:

> "Temptations, hidden snares
> often take us unawares,
> and our hearts are made to bleed
> for a thoughtless word or deed;
> and we wonder why the test
> when we try to do our best,
> but we'll understand it better by and by."[18]

But it's awfully hard to wait till "by and by." We live in "the here and now." Things happen *now*. And whatever God is doing,

---

[18] Charles Albert Tindley, "We'll Understand It Better By and By," 1905.

it's awfully hard to know for sure what it is that God is doing, specifically, right now.

On the other hand, maybe it's you who's being blessed, and the other guy who's not—or, at least, not as much as you. Maybe he—or she—is mad at you because things are going well for you— which, of course, can make *you* mad at *him*—or *her*—because you're just doing the best you can like everybody else.

Something is always getting in the way of our getting along with each other, it seems, no matter who's got the short end of the stick.

ॐ

And that's when God finally shows up on Cain's doorstep.

It's hard—and perhaps dangerous—to get mad at God, even when things aren't going right for you—or when they are, and everybody else is mad at you because of it. But there's always your brother or sister or *somebody* human around you—somebody human—and different—whether a little or a lot—to take your frustrations out on.

Of course, in the story, Cain's only got Abel. (It may be too early in the development of human psychology for Cain to realize that he can be mad at his momma and daddy, too.) Cain's only got his brother Abel to take his anger out on. But his brother will do well enough.

Except that God is against the idea. Cain couldn't get God to give his offering a "thumbs-up," but his hostility toward the only other person around gets Cain a clearly-defined, divine thumbs-down.

"Cain, My boy, don't do what you're thinking about doing to your brother," God says.

But God says it in a way that makes you think He's more concerned about what Cain is going to do to himself than about what Cain is planning to do to Abel. Sin went after Cain's parents in the form of a serpent: subtle, sly and suggestive. But sin takes on a different form as it takes Cain on. Sin is now a lion lying at

Cain's doorstep, competing with God for Cain's soul, crouching to leap into Cain's heart if Cain will not open his heart to God.

"Cain, My boy," says God, "think about what you're going to do to yourself if you decide to do to your brother what you shouldn't do. Think about what you're going to do to your relationship with Me if you destroy your relationship with your brother."

❧

Think about the fact that your relationship with God involves every other human being in existence. Think about the fact that God has entered into every relationship you have with another individual—whether the relationship is positive or negative—healthy or fractured.

Nothing you do or say or think or feel in relation to another person is unconnected to God. It's kind of like when Jesus tells a crowd of people, *"What you do to the least of these, my brothers, you do to me."*[19]

❧

And God tells Cain, on the brink of a disaster of Cain's own choosing: "You can do what is right, right now. You can do what is right. And you should, for your sake, as well as for the sake of the one you want to hurt. Because if you don't, you will hurt yourself as much as, if not more than, the person you are planning to hurt."

Maybe that's why Jesus said, *"And do not fear those who kill the body but cannot kill the soul. Rather fear him who can destroy both soul and body in hell."*[20] Cain will have more to fear from God if he takes his brother's life than Abel will have to fear from Cain if Cain kills him.

---

[19] Matthew 25:45, ESV.
[20] Matthew 10:28, ESV.

And Cain does kill him—Abel, his brother—his innocent brother—even after God warns him not to—even after God tells Cain what sin will do to him and with him, if and when he does the evil deed.

And it is evil. We all know that—which is why murder—of your brother or anyone else—is not the point of the story.

಄⸳ఄ

Jesus may have this story—and the point of it—in mind when He comes to the place in His Sermon on the Mount where He says, *"everyone who is angry with his brother will be liable to judgment; whoever insults his brother will be liable to the council; and whoever says, 'You fool!' will be liable to the hell of fire."*

God confronted Cain about his murderous intent before Cain committed murder. Jesus confronts the intent in those who have never committed the act.

಄⸳ఄ

Have you been angry at anyone lately? Have you insulted someone—or wanted to? Have you called anybody names—face to face or behind the back or just in your own mind?

Don't raise your hand—we're all guilty—to some degree—sooner or later. It is the way we are, and why we are—in our hearts—just like Cain.

God warns us—urges us—away from the open door where sin waits to pounce upon us. And so often—far too often—we will not back away from doing what we desire to do to others, in thought or word or deed. And we sin against God and man, and sin devours our lives like the hungry lion it is.

And it can happen right under God's nose, as it did with Cain. God went to see Cain about his hatred problem and Cain went right out after God spoke to him and did the exact opposite of what God told him to do.

And Cain did what he did, not so much because he didn't like his brother. Cain went after his brother because he wasn't happy about the way God was treating him and figured things would be better if his brother wasn't in the way. God would have to accept Cain and his offering because, after Abel was removed from the process, Cain's offering would be the only one offered.

৵৽৽৻

But Jesus says, *"if you are offering your gift at the altar and there remember that your brother has something against you, leave your gift there, before the altar, and go. First, be reconciled to your brother, and then come and offer your gift."*

God told Cain before he did the thing he should not do, "Don't do it!" But Cain did it anyway. And God still came back to Cain—first to confront Cain with His knowledge of what Cain had done—and then to endure Cain's indifference, lies and blatant disrespect as He pronounced the divine and natural curse on Cain that his actions had brought down upon him.

The one who killed his brother will now have to wander the earth looking for a family. The one who spilled his brother's blood on the ground—the ground that provided him food to feed himself and make an offering to God—will find the ground no longer willing to give up its bounty to him.

The sinner is now at odds with the people around him and the earth beneath his feet and the God above his head. He is now as defenseless in the world as his brother was with him. Cain now understands the true wages of sin,[21] and he cries out to the God he would not listen to when he could have spared his brother—and himself.

৵৽৽৻

---

[21] Romans 6:23.

And the God Who judged Cain guilty listens—and grants the murderer the mercy he would not grant his innocent brother. God places a mark upon Cain, required by Cain's guilt, but revealing of God's grace. It is the sign of God's continuing presence, despite the sin—and the seal of God's ongoing protection.

And we who are sinners like Cain—we who have sinned against God and our brothers and sisters—we may also bear a mark—a symbol that signifies both our guilt—and God's grace to overcome it. It is a mark traced in innocent blood across our hearts. We wear it around our necks and hang it on our walls and raise it in our churches.

And it says to us that, by and by, we *will* understand it better— when the eternal morning comes and our relationships with all our brothers and sisters and God Himself—relationships so marred by sin—will be restored to the state God intended. And we will be the covenant community He always meant for us to be. And all the Abels will welcome all the Cains back home to the family of God, through *"Jesus, the Mediator of a new covenant,"* Whose *"sprinkled blood,"* the Bible says, *"speaks a better word than the blood of Abel."*[22]

ॐ

---

22 Hebrews 12:24, ESV.

Genesis 12:1-4a RSV

¹ *Now the Lord said to Abram, "Go from your country and your kindred and your father's house to the land that I will show you. ² I will make of you a great nation, and I will bless you, and make your name great, so that you will be a blessing. ³ I will bless those who bless you, and the one who curses you I will curse; and in you all the families of the earth shall be blessed."*

⁴ *So Abram went, as the Lord had told him; and Lot went with him.*

ৰু•ৰ্ড

5.

The God Who Says "Go!"

Genesis 12:1-4a RSV

There are turning points in history. Sometimes you recognize them as they're happening: Dwight Eisenhower saying, "Go," to the June 6th D-Day invasion of Normandy,[23] or John Kennedy saying, "Let's go to the moon."[24]

Sometimes, a turning point isn't recognized as such until later, when the results have made it obvious. Anyone watching Christopher Columbus go west in his three little ships looking for China,[25] or watching William Shakespeare go off to London looking for work in the theatre,[26] would not have thought at the time, "The world will never be the same after this."

There are a number of turning points in the Bible. The greatest of all, of course, is the Crucifixion of Jesus Christ, *the* ultimate turning point in human history.[27] But there are others, and most of these are of the not-so-obvious kind: a harp-playing shepherd boy going to see his older brothers who are away fighting a war;[28] a

---

[23] June 6, 1944.
[24] September 12, 1962.
[25] August 3, 1492.
[26] Between 1585 and 1588, exact date unknown.
[27] A Friday in April, AD 31, 32, or 33.
[28] 1 Samuel 17.

fugitive from justice leaving the desert to go back to a still dangerous Egypt;[29] a childless old man leaving his home and going somewhere else, somewhere new.

❧❦

In each of these examples, history has turned on the decision of one person. Many people are affected—in some cases, the whole world—but it is the decision of one person that makes the difference.

What the Bible also makes clear is that these turning-point decisions are not made by the individual alone. They are the result of an individual responding to the call of God to go in a specific direction with his or her life.

Not every turning-point moment is recorded in the Bible or in the newspaper headlines. Each of us experience turning-point encounters with God, the God Who calls the unlikely and undeserving to serve His purpose and accomplish His will. And the examples found in scripture may serve you well if God's call to you is in any way like theirs. And I think it is.

❧❦

Consider the last example I mentioned: the old man leaving his home and going somewhere new. We know this man as Abraham. And his turning point encounter with God is related with remarkable simplicity and understatement in Genesis, Chapter 12.

Here is a divine call to journey into the unknown and the unfamiliar, wholly dependent on God. When God calls, everything can change—anything is possible.

Paul says in Romans[30] that Abraham is the father of us all. And we have much to learn from our father Abraham.

The call of God to Abraham is very personal.

---

[29] Exodus 4:19-20.
[30] Romans 4:16.

We aren't told how God speaks to Abraham. We don't know *how* Abraham knows it is God Who is giving him his marching orders.

We're just told that God is giving them—and Abraham knows He is—and Abraham obeys the command. God speaks to Abraham in such a way that Abraham knows it is God. And Abraham does what God tells him to do.

It is amazing what God can do with just one person—one obedient, faithful person. Abraham is just one person, but because Abraham goes when God says, "Go," God changes the world through him. God works salvation through individuals who are willing to go when God says to. Monumental things often start with a simple act of obedience.

❦

Let's be clear: To be "called" is no particular sign of merit. It is, however, a sign of God's grace. The response of Abraham is what makes him special to us. But notice that, at this point, Abraham is "Abram." He is not yet Abraham—not yet who he will become—even though he's already 75 years old. When Abraham goes as God tells him to, it is the turning point in his life—even at his age. It is the end of his past and the beginning of his future.

If God calls Abraham to a land God will show him, the reasonable inference is that God will share the journey to it (and through it) with him.

But "going with God" is no cakewalk. Neither Abraham nor his descendants are spared the hardships and heartaches of life by going obediently in response to the call of God.

There is disappointment and suffering in the course of the journey. But Abraham lives his life in fellowship with God and in confidence that God's promises will become a reality. From this point on, Abraham will always be on the move—but he will never be alone.

God calls "to." And God calls "from" as well.

41

Do not seek your security and satisfaction in life in comfortable places and people, apart from the will of God. God says to Abraham, "Leave everything that protects you and provides for you—everything that has formed your identity and supported your status. Leave what you know, and come with Me where you do not know, and are not known, but where you will know, and you will become known—as someone quite different from who you were, and who you certainly would have become, if you had not left the life from which I called you."

God will show you where He is taking you, if you will go when He calls.

ᐧᐁᐧ

And then there's "The Promise":
> "*I will show you the land…*
> **I will make you into a great nation…**
> *I will bless you…*
> *I will make your name great,*
> **and you will be a blessing.**
> *I will bless those who bless you…*
> *I will curse whoever curses you,*
> **and all peoples on earth**
> **will be blessed through you.**"

ᐧᐁᐧ

God makes promises. And God keeps His promises.

God's promise is part of His plan to build a new humanity to replace the old. The fulfillment of the promise is only possible in relationship, because God has chosen to fulfill His purpose (of which the Promise—with a capital "P"—is a part) in relationship.

God's Promise is not His permission for you to strive for goals you desire in life. It is God's gift to you beyond all your efforts. You may obtain everything in life you set your sights on. You may—or you may not. But you will *not* receive God's Promise unless you live your life in obedience to Him.

If you live your life in obedience to God's call, you will receive the Promise. Not *may*—will. The Promise is promised by God—under specific circumstances. The Promise is about God's graciousness and power, not your cleverness and drive.

The shape of the future is determined not simply by the One who speaks the Promise, but by the way the recipient responds to it. Although Abraham will never see this promised future, his response to God will shape it. What God promises you is more about those who will come after you than about you. The Promise to one is for the benefit of many.

You cannot ignore God's call and expect to receive the Promise anyway. The fulfillment of the Promise is the natural consequence of living your life obedient to the call. You cannot fulfill the Promise yourself, and God will not fulfill it if you are not heeding the call and living in right relationship with Him as He requires.

৵৹

When author Charles Dickens wrote the novel, *David Copperfield,* he set the story within the early years of Victorian England. He made his main character the narrator of his own life story. The very first words of the book have David Copperfield wonder: "Whether I shall turn out to be the hero of my own life, or whether that station will be held by anyone else...."[31]

Young people tend to wonder: "Who am I? Who will I become? Do I have a 'promising' future? What can I expect from God over the rest of my life?"

But those of us with a few—or more than a few—years under our belts tend to think otherwise. If we're wondering anything, it's

---

[31] Charles Dickens, *David Copperfield*, 1850.

likely to be, "Who have I become and how did I get to be the person I am? Am I done or is there any more to life for me?"

Of course, if you're like me, you're also wondering, "Where did I leave my glasses, wallet, keys or comb, and why did I come into this room just now?"

But even we can wonder, as long as we draw breath on this earth, "Is there anything else God has in mind for me? Is there anything left that is mine to do and no one else's?"

Abraham may have been wondering this, as his 75th birthday came and went in his familiar surroundings. But he wouldn't be wondering long, because God was about to call him from everything safe, comfortable and familiar, to go to a whole new world—a whole new life—an unknown world—and an uncertain life, except for the one essential certainty: God.

❧

If there is a message here for you—a lesson you are to learn and apply to your own life—it is not that you should renew your passport and put your house on the market—necessarily.

The message is that you should *not* consider God to be done with you, regardless of your age or physical condition or past achievements. Nor should you consider yourself exempt from God's call to rearrange your life and alter your priorities, just because you're well established in the life and lifestyle you prefer.

You are dealing with a God Who picks the most unlikely people to command, "Go!" You see, that's what God does: He appears to people out of the blue (His "blue," as a matter of fact) and commands them to "Go!"

God told Abraham to leave his home and go to a place that was totally alien to him to create a people for God. This same God told His only-begotten Son to leave His heavenly home and go to a place that was totally alienated from Him to redeem a people for God.[32]

What has God called you to go *from*? Where has God called you to go *to*? What will happen to you if you heed God's voice and go from where you have been to where He will show you to go?

The life to which God calls us is a pilgrimage. It is a life of faith and obedience, of sacrifice and suffering. It is also (and foremost) a life of fellowship with God and participation with Him in His redemptive purpose. It is a life filled with the promise of the blessings of God.

Accept the call.

Believe the Promise.

Wherever He sends you, go.

❧

---

[32] Philippians 2:5-8; John 3:16.

Genesis 12:1-7 ESV

¹ *Now the Lord said to Abram, "Go from your country and your kindred and your father's house to the land that I will show you. ² And I will make of you a great nation, and I will bless you and make your name great, so that you will be a blessing. ³ I will bless those who bless you, and him who dishonors you I will curse, and in you all the families of the earth shall be blessed."*

⁴ *So Abram went, as the Lord had told him, and Lot went with him. Abram was seventy-five years old when he departed from Haran. ⁵ And Abram took Sarai his wife, and Lot his brother's son, and all their possessions that they had gathered, and the people that they had acquired in Haran, and they set out to go to the land of Canaan. When they came to the land of Canaan, ⁶ Abram passed through the land to the place at Shechem, to the oak of Moreh. At that time the Canaanites were in the land. ⁷ Then the Lord appeared to Abram and said, "To your offspring I will give this land." So he built there an altar to the Lord, who had appeared to him.*

෫−෧

Mark 1:16-20 ESV

¹⁶ *Passing alongside the Sea of Galilee, [Jesus] saw Simon and Andrew the brother of Simon casting a net into the sea, for they were fishermen. ¹⁷ And Jesus said to them, "Follow me, and I will make you become fishers of men." ¹⁸ And immediately they left their nets and followed him. ¹⁹ And going on a little farther, he saw James the son of Zebedee and John his brother, who were in their boat mending the nets. ²⁰ And immediately he called them, and they left their father Zebedee in the boat with the hired servants and followed him.*

෫−෧

6.

The Call and the Promise

Genesis 12:1-7; Mark 1:16-20 ESV

If you are here today—here in this worship service, but also here in America—it is because, at some point in the past, someone in your family line left "the old country," whether east, west, north or south, and came here—to this country. For some, it was a parent or grandparent; for a few, it was you, yourself. For most of us, it was some ancient ancestor unknown to us, whose name is lost in the mist of time.

That's the physical reality.

But there is also a spiritual reality related to your being in this place today. You are here now—in this worship service—because a spiritual ancestor left his old country to journey to a new one, in a never-before-undertaken pilgrimage of faith. That ancestor is the same for all of us. His name is Abraham. He is the father of the family of faith to which we all belong. He was the first to hear God's call—and go.

One day, God called Abraham. And Abraham went, and his family followed him, and their descendants followed them, and here we are—thousands of years later—still following—still responding to God's call.

Abraham was called from his home north and east of the land that would one day become Israel. He did not know where he was going; he simply went when called, to see where God wanted him to be. It turned out that he was going to Canaan, the future Israel, the land that his people would one day possess. But all of that was in a promised, but unseen, future. For the time being, he was a pilgrim—a stranger in a foreign land—because God called and he went.

☜☞

It is a wonder that Abraham would go. The world in which he lived—the world of the Fertile Crescent—was remarkably sophisticated and cosmopolitan at that time—far more so than Canaan "next door." The evidence of archeology shows Abraham's homeland to have been peaceful, prosperous and socially progressive, supported by the stability of a common law and language. Business, science and the arts flourished. It was the most advanced civilization around—and would remain superior to anything that followed for many hundreds of years.[33]

In the world where Abraham was born and raised—before the advent of military empires—society rejected the rule of powerful individuals in favor of consensus government. And people assumed heaven operated the same way. They believed heaven was filled with many gods and none ruled over the others. There was no single or ultimate authority. And with no authority in heaven, there was no certainty to life on earth.[34]

But God was not willing for humanity to go on living in this misconception, and He revealed to one man that there is only one God—a God of power and might—Who rules heaven with absolute authority—and earth in the same way. And God called this one man, Abraham, out of the world of folly and into a new

---

[33] John Bright, *A History of Israel*, Third Edition, Philadelphia, PA: Westminster Press, 1981, pp. 23-33.
[34] Bright, pp.33-35.

world of faith. And for a time, Abraham alone bore the divine revelation of true reality—one man in all the world who carried in his heart and mind the first faint ember of faith's fire.

God called Abraham and made him some remarkable promises. But Abraham had to go—to obey God's call—before any of the promises were fulfilled. He would have to keep on going—all his life—to have all the promises fulfilled. And even then, the fulfillment would not come finally until generations after Abraham breathed his last and was carried to his grave.

৵৵

In fact, God's promises to Abraham are still being fulfilled, even today. God is fulfilling them in us. Abraham is our spiritual ancestor and we are the heirs in this generation of the promises God made for the first time to Abraham in his. And God's promises to Abraham are still paying off.

God promised Abraham that his descendants would be formed into a great nation—and so we have been. But do not look for confirmation to your identity cards; look in the Bible.

First Peter, Chapter 2 says, *"...you are a chosen race, a royal priesthood, a holy nation..."*[35] not because you were born in—or have come to—this country, but because you have heard and obeyed God's call to another "country," a far country, foreign to the ways of this world—a land of divine and remarkable promises.

God promised Abraham that his name would be made great. And are we not celebrating this first pilgrim of faith thousands of years later, while countless kings and conquerors lie dead and devalued, their names and titles long forgotten?[36] And because of Abraham, are we—here—not now called by a Name that is above every name, on earth and in heaven[37]—the name of a Descendant

---

[35] 1 Peter 2:9, NIV.
[36] See, for instance, "Ozymandias," a poem by Percy Bysshe Shelley, 1818.
[37] Philippians 2:10-11.

of Abraham born to fulfill God's promise to Abraham and all His spiritual descendants?[38]

God promised Abraham that Abraham would become a blessing that all the world would experience. And have we not seen this world transformed for good in the wake of the ongoing blessing of faith in the one true God that Abraham's first act of obedience set in motion?

⁂

But before God said, "Go to the land I will show you—the land of promise," God said, "Leave your country, your people and your father's household.

"Leave your country—the land you know and the familiar life you have built there.

"Leave your people—the social structures you have created or inherited and the culture you know so well.

"Leave your father's household—the place where you are protected and provided for—the organization that assures your status and power as a son—and all that you stand to inherit someday as a son."

To obey God's call, you must leave where you are to go where He leads. God said to Abraham and says to you, "Leave everything in the life you've gotten used to and go with Me to the life I have in mind for you."

It is a scary thing to set out on a journey whose end you cannot see—to put your faith in a God you have not known—and hope He will be faithful in return.

But Abraham considered the alternative—ignoring this God Who called him and living without the divine promises this God made him. And that option was even less acceptable.

Abraham would leave his life—his world—behind—and go. He would go at God's command. He would go in faith.

---

[38] Romans 4:23-25.

Abraham's obedience to "the *one* God" led him to abandon the many gods of his homeland. Abraham's obedience set events of faith in motion in the lives of his descendants that would usher in additional calls to Jacob[39] and Moses[40] and Joshua,[41] to Samuel[42] and David[43] and Isaiah[44] and Jeremiah[45] and Amos[46] and Hosea[47] and on and on, until finally, one day, God called, in the voice of a Man, to other men sitting in their boats, secure in the lives they had established for themselves.

And this God Incarnate gave the same command He had given to Abraham almost two thousand years before: *"Come, follow me."*

The Son of Abraham Who was also Son of God said, *"Follow me and I will make you fishers of men."*

A call and a promise.

And where were they going?

To the next village and all over the countryside. And farther still, to Jerusalem and Samaria and beyond, to Abraham's homeland and finally to Rome itself.[48]

�⋖

"Leave your boats and follow Me. Leave your nets and take up Mine."

"Where are we going?"

"Come and see."

"What about the life I've always known?"

"I'll give you a new one like nothing you've ever known before."

---

[39] Genesis 28:10-15.
[40] Exodus 3—4.
[41] Joshua 1:1-2.
[42] 1 Samuel 3:1-11.
[43] 1 Samuel 16:1-13.
[44] Isaiah 6:1-9.
[45] Jeremiah 1:4-10.
[46] Amos 7:14-15.
[47] Hosea 1:1-2.
[48] Acts 1:8; 28:16, 30-31.

"What do You promise in return?"

"Everything I promised Abraham and more. You will be part of a great spiritual nation of believers. Your names will be great, remembered and revered wherever those who have answered My call rehearse the story. You will be a blessing to the world. You will transform lives by mediating the power and presence of this one true God wherever you go, and everyone who hears and believes you will hear the call and receive the promise, too."

God called and they—like Abraham—heard and obeyed.

And God is still calling. And the God Who is in Christ,[49] and is Christ,[50] is still offering—promising—the miraculous. By yourself—apart from God—there is no promise in your life. *"Eat, drink and be merry"*[51] if you can; but you're on your own. Gather all you little gods around you—and all your little good luck charms—and hope for the best—right where you are. Enjoy everything your old familiar world has to offer with its sophisticated culture and consensus civilization—everything but the one true God.

Or follow in the footsteps of your spiritual ancestor Abraham and respond to the God Who calls and promises. Take up the Cross of the Christ Who calls you to discipleship[52] and promises you eternal life.[53]

The journey of faith for all humanity began with God's call to one man. Your faith journey begins when you answer God's call to you.

I promise.

But, more importantly, so does God.

☙❧

---

[49] 2 Corinthians 5:19.
[50] John 1:1.
[51] Luke 12:19, NIV.
[52] Matthew 16:24.
[53] John 3:36.

Genesis 15:1-7 ESV

¹ After these things the word of the Lord came to Abram in a vision: "Fear not, Abram, I am your shield; your reward shall be very great." ² But Abram said, "O Lord God, what will you give me, for I continue childless, and the heir of my house is Eliezer of Damascus?" ³ And Abram said, "Behold, you have given me no offspring, and a member of my household will be my heir." ⁴ And behold, the word of the Lord came to him: "This man shall not be your heir; your very own son shall be your heir." ⁵ And he brought him outside and said, "Look toward heaven, and number the stars, if you are able to number them." Then he said to him, "So shall your offspring be." ⁶ And he believed the Lord, and he counted it to him as righteousness.

ॐॐ

Romans 4:13-25 ESV

[13] For the promise to Abraham and his offspring that he would be heir of the world did not come through the law but through the righteousness of faith. [14] For if it is the adherents of the law who are to be the heirs, faith is null and the promise is void. [15] For the law brings wrath, but where there is no law there is no transgression.

[16] That is why it depends on faith, in order that the promise may rest on grace and be guaranteed to all his offspring—not only to the adherent of the law but also to the one who shares the faith of Abraham, who is the father of us all, [17] as it is written, "I have made you the father of many nations"—in the presence of the God in whom he believed, who gives life to the dead and calls into existence the things that do not exist. [18] In hope he believed against hope, that he should become the father of many nations, as he had been told, "So shall your offspring be." [19] He did not weaken in faith when he considered his own body, which was as good as dead (since he was about a hundred years old), or when he considered the barrenness of Sarah's womb. [20] No unbelief made him waver concerning the promise of God, but he grew strong in his faith as he gave glory to God, [21] fully convinced that God was able to do what he had promised. [22] That is why his faith was "counted to him as righteousness." [23] But the words "it was counted to him" were not written for his sake alone, [24] but for ours also. It will be counted to us who believe in him who raised from the dead Jesus our Lord, [25] who was delivered up for our trespasses and raised for our justification.

ॐ⋅ॐ

7.

The Impact of a Promise

Genesis 15:1-6; Romans 4:13-25 ESV

I am fascinated, from time to time, at how popular, secular movies stumble upon some deep, spiritual truth without even knowing it. For instance, in the *Matrix* movies[54] that were the rage some years ago, a man discovered to his amazement that he was living, not in one world, but two. In these movies, one of the worlds was a computer-generated simulation, and the other, apparently, was the "real" world—a world of which most people were completely unaware.

And here's the fascinating thing: There actually are two worlds—two realities—in which we live our lives. They co-exist in the same time and space, but they are separate realities—different dimensions of human existence. Neither is a simulation. Neither is computer generated. Both were generated long ago by the same Source: God. God created both, but He relates to each very differently.

The first world—or reality—He created at the beginning of time—earth and sky, day and night, plants and animals—and people who bore His image and soon chose to sin against Him and

---

54 Movies *The Matrix, The Matrix Reloaded, The Matrix Revolutions,* 1999-2009.

go their own way in this world God carefully and perfectly prepared for them.

The other world—the other reality—did not require a new planet to be formed or the universe around it to be rearranged. God called this new world into existence by calling one man out of all the men in the world and inviting him and his descendants to have a different relationship with Him.

And to this one man, God made promises—profound, and yet seemingly preposterous, promises—that the man had the freedom to believe or not. And when the man decided to believe the promises God make to him—even though God had not fulfilled them—a new world—a new reality for humanity—came into existence. The man who believed what God promised him was a man named Abraham. He lived in this new world God created in response to his faith in God's promise. And all of Abraham's descendants who believe in God's promise as he did, live in this new world, too—including you—if you believe.

☙❧

The world of faith looks very much the same as that other world in many ways. The sun comes up in the east each day and sets in the west. The laws of nature apply to one of these worlds just as they do to the other. We drive on the same roads and shop at the same grocery stores and live in the same neighborhoods as the people who live their lives in that other world.

But these are *not* the same world.

If you believe God—that He is continuing to fulfill the promise He made to Abraham in the lives of Abraham's descendants—you live in the world where God is, in fact, actively engaged in your life to fulfill His promise in you.

Yes, God makes the rain to fall on the just and the unjust[55]— especially if they have forgotten their umbrellas. But while people

---

[55] Matthew 5:45.

in that other world reject God and His availability for personal relationship and the special blessings that blossom out of such a relationship, you live in the world where God performs miracles and transforms lives and gives holy gifts and provides a sacred and sufficient "place" and opens a future for you where all His promises will be fulfilled for you.

Those who live in the world of disbelief do not believe that the world of faith exists. They cannot see it because God has chosen to make it visible only to the eyes of faith. They cannot see it; therefore, it cannot "be"—and never will be, unless they choose to believe and open the eyes of faith—kind of like that skeptic in the movie *Field of Dreams*[56] who, in the midst of a medical emergency, suddenly sees a reality he had been certain a moment before did not exist and asks, "Where did all these ballplayers come from?"

And every day, people who finally choose to believe are exclaiming in amazement, "Where did this other world come from?" And we say, "Welcome to Abraham's world—the world God created by faith—for faith."

❧

How did this one man, out of all the men—and women—in the world, become, along with his wife, Sarah, the founding father and mother of this new world? Was he better at believing than anybody else?

Not if you read the whole story. Abraham waited for God to fulfill His promise, but he didn't always wait patiently. He waited—and whined a lot about how long it was taking. He waited—but wanted—and tried, on occasion[57]—to "help God out" because what God promised seemed pretty hard to make happen the way God promised it.

It just says, "Abraham believed" God would do what He said He would do, and that was good enough for God. The Jewish

---

[56] Movie *Field of Dreams*, 1989.
[57] Genesis 16.

people—Abraham's physical descendants—exist today, despite Egyptian bondage and Babylonian exile, centuries of anti-Semitism and too many Holocausts to count—because, generation after generation, amid struggle, suffering and sorrow, there were those among them who believed that God would keep His word to Abraham and his descendants.

And one of those descendants—the Apostle Paul—saw in Jesus Christ and His Crucifixion and Resurrection the unique fulfillment of God's promise to Abraham, giving everyone the opportunity to become Abraham's spiritual descendant—by faith in Jesus—and to live in this other world of faith—Abraham's world.

ॐ

Of course, that other world—populated by people who don't, and perhaps won't, believe—has not been unaffected by Abraham and his choice so long ago to believe God. The fingerprints of the faith of former generations are all over that world and account for a great deal of the good that still resides within that world.

And in each generation, the believers like Abraham continuously urge those who reject faith to reconsider—to come in faith to this other, better world, where God is not the Stranger He is forced to be—or the Myth He is thought to be—over there.

The man in the *Matrix* movies was urged by those in the real world to give up the illusion of life in the world around him and become "Neo"—"New"—in theirs. Everyone in Abraham's world of faith is "new,"[58] because that's the life God promised to give everyone who believes in Him.

Believe—like Abraham did—and live in this new world with God.

ॐ

---

[58] Revelation 21:5.

Genesis 15:1-18 ESV

¹ After these things the word of the Lord came to Abram in a vision: "Fear not, Abram, I am your shield; your reward shall be very great."

² But Abram said, "O Lord God, what will you give me, for I continue childless, and the heir of my house is Eliezer of Damascus?" ³ And Abram said, "Behold, you have given me no offspring, and a member of my household will be my heir."

⁴ And behold, the word of the Lord came to him: "This man shall not be your heir; your very own son shall be your heir." ⁵ And he brought him outside and said, "Look toward heaven, and number the stars, if you are able to number them." Then he said to him, "So shall your offspring be." ⁶ And he believed the Lord, and he counted it to him as righteousness.

⁷ And he said to him, "I am the Lord who brought you out from Ur of the Chaldeans to give you this land to possess."

⁸ But he said, "O Lord God, how am I to know that I shall possess it?"

⁹ He said to him, "Bring me a heifer three years old, a female goat three years old, a ram three years old, a turtledove, and a young pigeon."

¹⁰ And he brought him all these, cut them in half, and laid each half over against the other. But he did not cut the birds in half. ¹¹ And when birds of prey came down on the carcasses, Abram drove them away.

¹² As the sun was going down, a deep sleep fell on Abram. And behold, dreadful and great darkness fell upon him.

¹³ Then the Lord said to Abram, "Know for certain that your offspring will be sojourners in a land that is not theirs and will be servants there, and they will be afflicted for four hundred years. ¹⁴ But I will bring judgment on the nation that they serve, and afterward they shall come out with great possessions. ¹⁵ As for you, you shall go to your fathers in peace; you shall be buried in a good old age. ¹⁶ And they shall come back here in the fourth generation, for the iniquity of the Amorites is not yet complete."

¹⁷ When the sun had gone down and it was dark, behold, a smoking fire pot and a flaming torch passed between these pieces.

[18] On that day the Lord made a covenant with Abram, saying, "To your offspring I give this land, from the river of Egypt to the great river, the river Euphrates…."

৯•৩

8.

What It Takes to Be Righteous

Genesis 15:1-18 ESV

Unless you just happen to be into archaic religious rituals, the story of Abraham's encounter with God in Genesis 15 is going to strike you as something out of *The Twilight Zone*:[59] visions and voices—star gazing and future predicting—and enough ritual killing of animals to set PETA[60] on the warpath. And yet, wrapped up in all the weirdness of the story is an event so important that you can't afford to miss it.

Abraham and his wife, Sarah, are way too old to be making babies, and yet Abraham hears God telling him that God is going to create a whole nation—and radically change the world—through a baby Abraham and Sarah will make. If they ever made a baby, it would be very important—huge—but there's something even more important than that.

Even more important than a miracle of biologically mind-boggling proportions is the fact that Abraham believes God's promise that God is going to make this miracle happen—and that God, in turn, defines Abraham's faith in God's promise as righteousness. Because Abraham believes God, Abraham is "okay"

---

[59] Television series, 1959-1964.
[60] People for the Ethical Treatment of Animals.

with God—fully acceptable to God. And from this point on, Abraham will live his life connected to God rather than separated from God.

Let's take that and run with it.

Genesis 15 is really about the two basic options in life: living your life with God and living your life without God. And you all have a lot more of your lives ahead of you than most of the rest of us do.[61] But the question is: which life?

Imagine for a moment what your life will be if you believe God—day after day, year after year—until you reach the end—the end here, anyway. It will certainly be different from the life you will have if you do not believe God.

Notice, I did not say, "Believe *in* God." God is not interested in your intellectual opinion about His existence, something you can sit back and contemplate in splendid isolation. God makes promises that, when believed, form the basis for relationship with Him—a personal and corporate, covenant relationship.

If you choose to believe the promises God makes, God pronounces you acceptable to Him and eligible to live your life within the circle of His love and guidance and grace. God treats you differently when you believe Him—believe what He promises you. Not because He likes you better, but because your belief opens you to God and allows Him to work out your life with you and for you.

If you could only see what your life will be, given your choice! If only you were able to compare the two people you will become, across the course of your life!

You can't, of course, except as God lays it out for you.

---

[61] The sermon was preached on a Sunday when a large college choir was visiting and providing special music throughout the service. The sermon was directed primarily to these students.

God laid it out for Abraham: "Abraham, this is what I'm going to do for you. Will you trust Me to do what I've promised you?"

ॐ⌁ঞ

So, which life will you live?

You may be different, but most people who are your age, and in your environment, are experiencing a lot of pressure not to believe. Believing God is not considered smart or sophisticated or cool. And if your background taught you differently, and you can't let that go, the message of modern society is, "Put off making a decision. Other things are more important right now—and more fun."

But there are some things you need to know. One is that the longer you go before you believe God, the harder it will become for you to believe Him. Another is that to make no decision about believing God is, to God, a decision *not* to believe Him.

Another is that those who ridicule the idea of believing God are exercising just as much faith in the idea that God does not exist or cannot be trusted as those whose faith in God they disparage.

God's promises can't be "proven" false any more than they can be "proven" true. The truth is that there will always be enough uncertainty to support your doubts, but there will also always be enough evidence to support your faith.[62] Trust God and God will prove your faith well-founded in the course of your on-going life of faith.

ॐ⌁ঞ

Think how much hinged on which way Abraham would respond to God. Think how much depends on what you do with God's promises to you.

---

[62] This classic formulation of the argument for faith in God is found in *Pensées*, a collection of fragmentary ideas by French philosopher and mathematician Blaise Pascal, first published posthumously, and translated by John Walker in 1688.

Believe, or blow it off—what impact will your faith or lack of it have on your life and the lives of your family and friends and of people yet unborn?

Abraham believed God and God called it "righteousness."

Does that mean that Abraham became perfect?

Not as we define it.

But Abraham did become perfectly acceptable to God—as we do today when we believe God's promise to us, expressed now in Jesus Christ. Whatever Abraham's sins and shortcomings, before and after the encounter in Genesis 15, because he believed God, Abraham became exactly who God wanted him to be.

The same thing happened to the Apostle Paul in the New Testament. Paul was wasting his life—ruining his life. Then the Lord came to him in a vision and Paul believed what he was told.[63] From that point on, Paul lived his life with God, not against God.

৵৽৹

Don't misunderstand: Believing God does not make the difference in the life you live, but it does allow God to make the difference.

The question to ask yourself today is "Can I trust God?"

The question God asks you is "*Will* you trust Me?"

If you do not trust God, you do not live in a different world from those who do. You live in this world, but in a different way— the wrong way—a way that God did not design for you and that will not result in your realizing the fullness of God's promises.

The poet Robert Frost wrote about two roads diverging in a wood, only one of which he could follow.[64]

Two lives diverge—your lives—your life *believing* God and your life *without* God—and you can choose but one way to follow.

---

[63] Acts 9:1-22.
[64] Robert Frost, "The Road Not Taken," 1920.

Each day, the gap between them will grow wider. You cannot straddle. You cannot live them both.

Believe God and live the better life—your life with God.

৶৽৻

Genesis 17:15-19 ESV

¹⁵ And God said to Abraham, *"As for Sarai your wife, you shall not call her name Sarai, but Sarah shall be her name.* ¹⁶ *I will bless her, and moreover, I will give you a son by her. I will bless her, and she shall become nations; kings of peoples shall come from her."* ¹⁷ Then Abraham fell on his face and laughed and said to himself, *"Shall a child be born to a man who is a hundred years old? Shall Sarah, who is ninety years old, bear a child?"* ¹⁸ And Abraham said to God, *"Oh that Ishmael might live before you!"* ¹⁹ God said, *"No, but Sarah your wife shall bear you a son, and you shall call his name Isaac. I will establish my covenant with him as an everlasting covenant for his offspring after him."*

᪥

Luke 1:26-35 ESV

²⁶ In the sixth month the angel Gabriel was sent from God to a city of Galilee named Nazareth, ²⁷ to a virgin betrothed to a man whose name was Joseph, of the house of David. And the virgin's name was Mary. ²⁸ And he came to her and said, *"Greetings, O favored one, the Lord is with you!"* ²⁹ But she was greatly troubled at the saying, and tried to discern what sort of greeting this might be. ³⁰ And the angel said to her, *"Do not be afraid, Mary, for you have found favor with God.* ³¹ *And behold, you will conceive in your womb and bear a son, and you shall call his name Jesus.* ³² *He will be great and will be called the Son of the Most High. And the Lord God will give to him the throne of his father David,* ³³ *and he will reign over the house of Jacob forever, and of his kingdom there will be no end."*

³⁴ And Mary said to the angel, *"How will this be, since I am a virgin?"*

³⁵ And the angel answered her, *"The Holy Spirit will come upon you, and the power of the Most High will overshadow you; therefore the child to be born will be called holy—the Son of God."*

᪥

9.

Impossible Child

Genesis 17:15-19; Luke 1:26-35 ESV

Most of the time, when people talk about an "impossible child," they mean a child who's hard to discipline—a behavioral problem. At least, that's how my teachers—at school and at church—used the term when they would talk with my parents about me when I was a child.

But that's another story.

⇛⇚

When the Bible talks about "impossible children"—and it talks about more than one—it doesn't mean "hard to handle."

In a time as far before the birth of Jesus as we are after it, God promised Abraham that his wife, Sarah, would give birth to a son.

"Impossible!" Abraham snorted. "Ninety-year-old women can't have babies!" And when Sarah heard that God was predicting—promising—a pregnancy for her, she had the same reaction—though she tried to deny it when God called her out on it.

They were all agreed: Sarah having a child at her age was impossible. They all agreed—except God.

"You laugh when I tell you what I am going to do?" says God. "Fine! When this 'impossible' child is born, you call him 'Laughter'"[65]

And then, the impossible happened.[66]

And not only was a child born when it seemed humanly impossible, but the child became the otherwise impossible means to the fulfillment of promises so vast and momentous that they, too, would have seemed impossible—to Abraham, Sarah, Isaac and their descendants—had God not been the One Who made them—and made them come true…

                                         ❧❧

…which is exactly what's happening when, all those many centuries later, a young Jewish girl, a virgin—betrothed but not yet married—a descendent of Abraham and Sarah through the child it was impossible for Sarah to bear (until she did)—a Jewish girl halfway in history between Sarah and us—experiences her own divine visitation, and receives her own supernatural promise that she will give birth to her own impossible Child—a Child even more impossible than the one Sarah had been promised and produced.

At least with Abraham and Sarah, impossibly old as they were to conceive a child together, there was a father's seed and a mother's egg. With Mary—who is certainly a more appropriate age for having children—there will be no man involved in the conception of the Child she will carry in her womb, which makes conception impossible, of course, even in our own high-tech era of artificial insemination.

God will merely "tell" Mary's body to conceive. He will speak this impossible Child into existence just as He spoke the first man—and woman—into existence—along with their world—in the Beginning.[67]

---

[65] The name "Isaac" means "laughter" in Hebrew.

[66] Genesis 21:1–7.

[67] Genesis 1:26-27.

And God has a name for this impossible Child, just as He had a name for the child it was impossible for Sarah to bear. God's messenger to Mary tells her to call her Child: "Jesus—Savior."

இ•ઉ

Isaac's name was a reminder at first of the bitter laughter of two people who had been around so long that they could not believe God could or would do the impossible. And then "Isaac" became the name of their joyful response to the child whose birth transformed their experience of the present and their perception of their past and their expectations for the future.

Their impossible child was proof that God would fulfill all the promises He had made for the future of their family.

They did not live to see God do the impossible things He promised to do through Isaac.[68] They did not live to see their son sire a nation. They did not live to see the many kings who descended from him. They did not live to see the Savior of the world Who claimed them as His ancestors, both by flesh and by faith.[69] But they were told by God that He would give them an impossible child, and finally, they believed God, and, because of their faith, all the other impossible things happened as well.

இ•ઉ

The promises God is making to Mary—of the Child she will carry, though it is impossible—and of the impossible things this impossible Child will do—are not just for the benefit of her family, as with Abraham and Sarah—not just for building a handful of people into a nation. God is promising the Savior of the world— to the world. Through her—Mary—all the world will be blessed.

Of course, at the very moment God's angel speaks to Mary of the impossible things that are about to happen—of the Savior of the world to be conceived within her—most of the world thinks

---

[68] Hebrews 11:11-13.
[69] Romans 4:13-21.

there is already a much stronger claimant for that title: Caesar Augustus. And compared to the great and god-like Caesar, ruling the vast expanses of his empire from the incomparable capital of Rome, the idea that any Jew, peasant or aristocrat, could do anything that would affect the whole world, or even get its attention, would seem absolutely impossible.

And in that regard at least, nothing much has changed, despite all that has happened since Gabriel went to Galilee to let a young girl named Mary in on the impossible things God was about to do. You and I live in a time when more things are humanly possible than at any time in the history of the world. And yet people are more convinced than ever that what is humanly *im*-possible is also impossible for God.

In fact, there are more people alive today than ever before who believe that the very existence of God is impossible. Mention God in public in any serious or reverential way and you will be met by the original Abrahamic response: derisive laughter. "How can anybody with half a brain believe there is a god in this day and age?! It's impossible and everybody knows it!"

And this is the world—these are the people—to whom God announces the coming of His impossible Child and the fulfillment of promises so impossibly wonderful that anyone who will believe Him will go from cynicism to celebration.

☙•❧

Look at God's pattern: God tells people the impossible things He's going to do—the impossible Child He has brought into the world and will bring into their lives. He tells people—and invites them to believe in—the impossible, before He has accomplished it. And when they do, then God does the impossible. God brings the Isaacs and the Samuels[70] and the John the Baptists[71]—and

---

[70] 1 Samuel 1:19–20.
[71] Luke 1:57–66.

finally, Jesus (of Whom there is only one)—into the world to bless the world, and, ultimately, to save the world from itself.

Funny thing about these impossibilities God announces and then brings into being: If you believe God when He tells you He is going to do impossible things in your life—He does them.

If you doubt—if you laugh it off—blow God's good news off and don't believe—He doesn't do what He can do, and would do, if you believed as He calls you to—if you believed and then waited for the fulfillment of His promises.

God promised Sarah a child and all the promises that went with him. And, impossible as it was, Sarah bore Isaac. And her life was blessed forever after.

God promised Mary that she would give birth—as a virgin— to the Savior of the world.

And impossible as this was even to imagine, Mary told the angel, *"Let it be to me according to your word."* And, according to another Gospel, *"…the Word became flesh and dwelt among us…."*[72]

Impossible!

ও◦ড়

And yet, all who believe the promises of God revere Mary to this day—and, as it happens, have been given *"power to become children of God."*[73]

It was impossible for God to establish and preserve His covenant people from Abraham and Sarah throughout the centuries, so that the Messiah could come forth from these people, and this covenant, as God promised. It was impossible for Jesus to be born—as God promised. It was impossible for Jesus to be raised from the dead—as God promised. It is impossible for Jesus to come back to earth as the eternal King Who will grant eternal life to those who believe in Him, and decree eternal punishment to those who are convinced that these things are impossible and so

---

[72] John 1:14, RSV.
[73] John 1:12, RSV.

live their lives committed only to the humanly possible, confident in the impossibility of the impossible.

But this is a God Who is not hampered or deterred by man's sense of what is impossible.

And we believe His promises of the impossible things to come because we have seen the impossible things God has brought to pass already, even to this day.

A virgin will conceive and bear a Son.

Biologically impossible.

The Child will be the Savior of the world.

Functionally impossible.

This Jewish peasant will be great.

Socially impossible.

This human being will be the Son of the Most High God.

Theologically impossible.

God will give Him the throne of His ancestor, King David.

Politically impossible.

He will reign over the house of Jacob forever.

Logically impossible.

Of His kingdom, there will be no end.

Conceptually impossible.

రెడ్జు

And yet, that's what happened—and is happening—and will happen. But if you do not believe it when God tells you, it won't happen *to you*. It is impossible for this Child—this Christ Child—to be born *in you* if you do not believe God when He promises to put Jesus in your heart and life. It is impossible to live a new, transformed life in Christ if you do not believe that God can and will give it to you as He promised. If you wait until you can get your hands or mind around something that doesn't seem so impossible, you will miss out on all the impossible things God is promising you—and is prepared to provide you.

We did not read to the end of the angel's conversation with Mary this morning. Before he was done, Gabriel told her one of the greatest truths of the universe: *"…with God, nothing will be impossible."*[74]

God does the impossible—all the time. There is no child that He cannot bring to life.

There is no life that He cannot transform through the Child Whose coming at Christmas was supposed to be impossible but wasn't.

Take a lesson from Mary—and from Sarah: Believe God, no matter how impossible it may seem, and see the impossible happen in your life—over and over again, forever and ever, Amen.

ॐ

---

[74] Luke 1:37, RSV.

Genesis 22:1-19 ESV

¹ *After these things God tested Abraham and said to him, "Abraham!" And he said, "Here I am." ² He said, "Take your son, your only son Isaac, whom you love, and go to the land of Moriah, and offer him there as a burnt offering on one of the mountains of which I shall tell you." ³ So Abraham rose early in the morning, saddled his donkey, and took two of his young men with him, and his son Isaac. And he cut the wood for the burnt offering and arose and went to the place of which God had told him. ⁴ On the third day Abraham lifted up his eyes and saw the place from afar. ⁵ Then Abraham said to his young men, "Stay here with the donkey; I and the boy will go over there and worship and come again to you." ⁶ And Abraham took the wood of the burnt offering and laid it on Isaac his son. And he took in his hand the fire and the knife. So they went both of them together. ⁷ And Isaac said to his father Abraham, "My father!" And he said, "Here I am, my son." He said, "Behold, the fire and the wood, but where is the lamb for a burnt offering?" ⁸ Abraham said, "God will provide for himself the lamb for a burnt offering, my son." So they went both of them together.*

⁹ *When they came to the place of which God had told him, Abraham built the altar there and laid the wood in order and bound Isaac his son and laid him on the altar, on top of the wood. ¹⁰ Then Abraham reached out his hand and took the knife to slaughter his son. ¹¹ But the angel of the Lord called to him from heaven and said, "Abraham, Abraham!" And he said, "Here I am." ¹² He said, "Do not lay your hand on the boy or do anything to him, for now I know that you fear God, seeing you have not withheld your son, your only son, from me." ¹³ And Abraham lifted up his eyes and looked, and behold, behind him was a ram, caught in a thicket by his horns. And Abraham went and took the ram and offered it up as a burnt offering instead of his son. ¹⁴ So Abraham called the name of that place, "The Lord will provide"; as it is said to this day, "On the mount of the Lord it shall be provided."*

¹⁵ *And the angel of the Lord called to Abraham a second time from heaven ¹⁶ and said, "By myself I have sworn, declares the Lord, because you have done this and have not withheld your son, your only son, ¹⁷ I will surely bless you, and I will surely multiply your offspring as the stars of heaven and as the sand*

that is on the seashore. And your offspring shall possess the gate of his[j] enemies, [18] and in your offspring shall all the nations of the earth be blessed, because you have obeyed my voice." [19] So Abraham returned to his young men, and they arose and went together to Beersheba. And Abraham lived at Beersheba.

❧

10.

Sacrificing Isaac

Genesis 22:1-19 ESV

A lot of people say they want to know God's will for their lives. Maybe they shouldn't.

God revealed His will to Abraham one day: *"Take your son, your only son, Isaac, whom you love, and...sacrifice him as a burnt offering...."*

Maybe Abraham had been praying, "Lord, show me Your will for my life."

God showed him, all right!

Now, in this case, you know more than Abraham knows. You know that God is testing Abraham, whatever you think of the test. Abraham only knows that God has told him to do the last thing on earth Abraham would ever want to do. God may show you His will, but it doesn't mean you're going to like it.

*"Take your son...*the child I promised you...the child you waited for all your life, whose birth came like the greatest miracle of all time...the child upon whom all My other promises, and all your hopes and dreams, depend.... Take this child—this Isaac—and sacrifice him."

Abraham doesn't just love this child; Abraham's whole future is riding on him. Abraham *needs* this child. Abraham desperately wants him to live. Isaac is Abraham's unique, one of a kind, son.

But the next morning, Abraham gets up and gets about God's will for his life—the will he knows, but surely wishes he didn't.

The Bible tells us everything Abraham does and nothing about what he's thinking or how he's feeling. It doesn't matter—Abraham knows God's will for his life and that's what he's doing.

Saddle up the donkey. Cut the wood. Gather up a few servants and the son to be sacrificed—and get on down the road.

Sometimes, you want to be "in God's will;" sometimes you just want to get it over with.

ॐ•ॐ

Abraham is going to do God's will, but every minute he is going, he *is* doing God's will. In Abraham's mind, Isaac may already be dead. God has directed that the boy be sacrificed. Abraham is acting obediently. This suggests he has an obedient spirit. It is a matter of trust.

Sacrifice Isaac. That's the will God has revealed to him—the will that drives him and those with him—including Isaac—day after day, until they come to the mountain God has chosen. And then Abraham and Isaac—the sacrificer and the sacrifice—the two of them—go on, up the mountain, together. And by now, even Isaac has figured out that things are different this time: "Father, where's the sacrificial lamb?"

What can Abraham say?

What he does say is, *"God himself will provide the lamb."*

In other words: "This is all God's will—not mine." What Abraham doesn't say is that it is God's will that you, Isaac, be sacrificed to Him. Abraham is doing God's will because God has revealed to Abraham what that will is.

Abraham is faithful to the will of God, but he also has faith in this God to work His divine will in a way Abraham cannot imagine, to achieve the divine purpose for which Isaac was promised and provided by God to Abraham.

You know it's a test, but you also know that Abraham doesn't know that. And so you watch with fascination as the old father goes methodically about the business of destroying everything he has to hold on to in this life—preparing to give his beloved son back to the God Who gave the boy to him in the first place.

Whatever is going on in his heart and mind, Abraham is obedient to the God Who has told him what he is to do: Pile up the stones—pile on the wood—tie up the boy and place him on the primitive altar—raise the knife—and strike home!

"No!"

It is not the will of God that this beloved son be a sacrifice this day on this hill.

❦

It was God's will that Abraham be *willing* to sacrifice Isaac— perhaps that Abraham had already sacrificed Isaac to God in his heart—just as God had instructed him to do. But God now knows what He wanted to know about Abraham. God now knows that Abraham is faithful, first of all, to God. Abraham will do the will of God, whatever it is.

And Abraham knows something about God in a way he did not know it before: God provides. Because Abraham was willing to sacrifice Isaac, God provided a substitute—an acceptable substitute. Abraham was called to sacrifice, but God provided the sacrifice.

God knows He can trust Abraham, and Abraham knows he can trust God. God knows He can use Abraham—and his descendants—as partners in the working out of His divine purpose—and Abraham and his descendants know that God will work His will through them.

❦

And through you.

What happens when you pray that God reveal His will for your life, and He does, and it isn't the "peace that passes understanding,"[75] or joy that knows no bounds?[76]

Or you don't pray to know God's will and He reveals it anyway. God reveals His will and this time you don't know it's a test. This time, God simply tells you to sacrifice your "Isaac."

๑๛

What am I talking about?

Let me give you an example.

Many years ago, my wife and I were attending a retreat for clergy and their spouses. There were dozens of couples there, all strangers to us. The first night, we were divided into small groups to get to know each other better.

One older couple revealed that they were in serious conflict. They had come to the retreat as a last try to save their marriage. The husband had entered into an agreement with a member of their church that was financially beneficial to the couple, but required the wife to take on, for an indefinite period of time, responsibilities beyond her ability to manage. He did not want to lose the benefit, and she could not cope with the pressure the arrangement created for her.

One of the ministers in the group offered to counsel with them. After listening to both, he suggested to the husband that to save the marriage—which was his primary obligation before God—he should consider whether God wanted him to "sacrifice Isaac," to terminate the agreement for the good of the marriage, and trust that God would provide for them despite the loss of the financial benefit that would result. To the husband, the agreement was a gift from God to secure their future. But he chose to give it up, and in so doing, he saved his marriage.

---

[75] Philippians 4:7.
[76] 1 Peter 1:8.

80

God is gracious beyond measure and blesses us with all good things. But God calls us, not, primarily, to enjoy His generosity, but to serve His purpose. Like Abraham, you and I are called, first of all, to be faithful—to believe in the promises of God and live obediently in response to the will God reveals to us. God loves us because of *His* nature, not ours. But His will for us is to participate with Him in the work of redemption, which we can only do when we are obedient to Him—as Abraham was—even to the point of sacrificing anything that competes for our loyalty and commitment.

To become a part of this fellowship, many of us had to sacrifice a beloved Isaac. We had to give up a cherished dream—something we had experienced as a tremendous blessing from God that we expected to enrich us spiritually in the future. But there came a day when God said, "Take it and sacrifice it."

Before God spoke, we could not have imagined it. And then God made it a matter of faithfulness to Him.

But that isn't the only example. All of us who are committed to living faithfully before the God Who has called us to discipleship will have been tested by God. And we will be tested again.

"Sacrifice this," says the God of Abraham. "Do not trust in things—even the things I give you. Trust in Me. Do not look upon My blessings as the goal of your relationship with Me. The relationship is the goal. Anything else may be sacrificed if required."

And you may have sacrificed many beloved things over the course of your life with God.

But just as God demands your complete and continuing trust and faithfulness, He is also completely and continually faithful to provide for you.

Abraham was right. When Isaac asked, "Where is the thing we need to do God's will?"

"God will provide it," he said.

Because we were willing to sacrifice what God called for, God has provided us a new and more glorious fellowship. Because you have been willing, when God required, to let go of things that gave you comfort or confidence, God has been able and willing to provide you greater comfort and deeper confidence and an assurance of your privileged place in His love and His work.

God was testing Abraham to see if He could trust him. God does the same with us. If we trust Him—if we believe His promises and obey His commands—we pass His test.

But can we trust God? Can you trust a God Who tells you to sacrifice your "Isaac," the thing you cherish most?

Well, you need to remember that your God is a Father Who took His own Son—His only begotten and beloved Son—up a mountain of sacrifice and did what He commanded—but did not require—Abraham to do. God sacrificed His "divine Isaac," Jesus Christ, the ultimate and eternal Son, fulfilling God's promise to Abraham and all his children.

As you go to make the sacrifice God calls you to make, and you find yourself asking, "Where is the lamb for the offering?" the answer remains the same: *"God will provide the lamb for the offering."* *God has* provided the Lamb— *"the Lamb of God who takes away the sins of the world."*[77]

"Take your Isaac and sacrifice him," says God. "Show Me that you trust Me and will obey Me—and you will find Me faithful in return: *My grace is sufficient for you....*[78] I will *supply all your need."*[79]

❧

---

[77] John 1:29, RSV.
[78] 2 Corinthians 12:9, NIV.
[79] Philippians 4:19, KJV.

11.

The Rebekah Project

Genesis 24 RSV

We have come to the time in the service when I am supposed to preach you a sermon. No matter what I might say to you, some of you would pay attention; others would not. Some of you would find the message relevant to your life situation—perhaps even useful. Others would quickly judge it off the mark and dismiss it from your minds. And the truth is that every sermon isn't for everybody every week.

Today, the sermon isn't for most of you, intentionally. Or to put it another way: The sermon today is only for a few of you.

This morning, the sermon is about a man on a mission. And the sermon is *for* the single men among us who are on the same mission—or should be—whether they realize it or not. The mission is to find and acquire a proper wife.

The Bible, God's divine revelation, provides instruction to us regarding a great many aspects of our lives, and not just the spiritual parts, because the spiritual is inseparable in our make-up as human beings from the physical and the social. The Bible even talks in a number of places about how God intends for a proper wife to be found.

One very useful example, unfortunately, fits the description I offered the last time I stood before you. It's one of those passages about "strange and ancient customs from a faraway land."

The passage is Genesis, Chapter 24, and the mission it describes is finding an acceptable wife for Isaac, Abraham's son and heir to the promise God made to Abraham. Let me read a few verses to set the stage. We will begin at the beginning of Genesis 24.

෨ඏ

¹ Abraham was now old and well advanced in years, and the LORD had blessed him in every way. ² He said to the chief servant in his household, the one in charge of all that he had, "Put your hand under my thigh. ³ I want you to swear by the LORD, the God of heaven and the God of earth, that you will not get a wife for my son from the daughters of the Canaanites, among whom I am living, ⁴ but will go to my country and my own relatives and get a wife for my son Isaac."

And then in verse 7, Abraham says,

"The LORD, the God of heaven, who brought me out of my father's household and my native land and who spoke to me and promised me on oath, saying, 'To your offspring I will give this land'—he will send his angel before you so that you can get a wife for my son from there."

෨ඏ

There's more to the story, of course, but before we read any farther, I suppose, we need to take on the question of the relevance of this story to the wife-seekers among us today. There are some seemingly reasonable objections you could make to letting these strange and ancient customs be the guiding principles in a project as important as finding an acceptable wife in 21ˢᵗ Century America.

For instance: "This isn't how young men get wives anymore."

How *do* young men in our modern society acquire their wives today?

I admit I don't keep up with all the latest trends—I haven't been looking for a wife in a long time. I'm quite satisfied with the wife I've got—and she says I'd better be!

But I did see recently on TV where a fellow is going to have three different women move into his home, each for a week, to see which one he likes best—as a national audience of millions looks on. The preview for this new series hinted that all may not have gone smoothly in this selection process.

Imagine!

I also hear that people "discover" one another in cyber chat rooms, falling madly in love based solely on what unknown individuals type on their computer screens.

And then there are cryptic personal ads you can put in the newspaper and automated dating services. Why would a guy today be interested in the biblical way to find and acquire a wife when he's got all these modern processes available?

The answer may be that timeless biblical principles are still better than our modern alternatives. After all, are the results of the latest fads for finding a wife producing better results than God's way? Are marriages resulting from the "modern methods" happier and healthier unions than those that follow the guidance of scripture? Is the state of the family in America today better than it's ever been before? If the modern process is superior, shouldn't the result be superior, too?

∾

"The Bible talks about *old* people *arranging* marriages for their children! What's wrong with just 'falling in love'?"

Twenty-five years of performing weddings and doing marriage counseling has taught me two things. The first is that *everybody* gets married today because they fall in love. The second is that before long a whole lot of these "married-for-love" couples fall so far out of love that they will go to remarkable lengths to make life hell for each other.

A few folks in the Bible get married because they love each other. A whole lot more decide to—or come to—love each other *because* they got married. And the truth is that *all* marriages are "arranged" by *somebody*, even today, and the bride and groom aren't always the only ones doing the arranging (regardless of what they think).

Yes, the biblical way of finding a wife is different. And no, it doesn't have a lot of support in our modern culture.

But maybe you ought to have a look anyway, so you'll have a basis for comparison, if nothing else. And if it will help, where the wife-seeker in Genesis is a wise and trusted servant of the future husband's father, you can apply the principles to yourself—if you are doing your own wife-seeking.

So what can you learn from "The Rebekah Project," the campaign to secure a suitable wife for Isaac, the son of Abraham—the son who personifies the Promise?

❧

Abraham, the head of the family, understands how much depends on finding and acquiring for his son a good and proper wife. Isaac may not understand. You are more likely to look for a proper wife if you have some sense of what is at stake, rather than if you are driven only by your physical desire, or your emotional need, or the social expectations being pressed upon you.

The finding and acquiring of a proper wife is an essential step in passing on to a new generation the blessings God has given you—and fulfilling the promises God has made to His family of faith, in and through His Son Jesus Christ. When a man "acquires" a wife (the term used in Genesis 24), he adds to the structure of civilization. When a man merely generates new people with a woman who is not his wife, that man takes away from the structure of society and pushes human community farther down the path to barbarism.

Abraham put his most mature, most responsible, and most trusted man on this project. There was nothing more important for the future of his family than this one mission.

If you are a single man, you should approach your "Rebekah Project" with the most mature, responsible, and trustworthy dimensions of your personality. *Nothing* you do in life will be as important, or have as great an impact on your future, and on the well-being of generations of your descendants, as the wife you acquire—with the single exception of your faith commitment to Jesus Christ.

The wife-seeker in Genesis 24 understands that *finding* a woman qualified to be a proper wife is a sign of God's kindness and faithfulness—not just to the groom, but to his family as well. You should ask God to guide you in your search for a wife, and to grant you success, not just in finding a wife—which for some young men might be considered a significant accomplishment in and of itself—but in finding, and recognizing, and opening your heart to, a *proper* wife.

In fact, maybe Jesus' admonition to *"seek first the Kingdom of God and His righteousness"* applies even to the search for a wife, with the promise that *"all these things shall be added unto you"*[80] applying as well.

Let's go back to the story and pick it up at verse 10.

❧

[10] Then the servant took ten of his master's camels and left, taking with him all kinds of good things from his master. He set out for Aram Naharaim and made his way to the town of Nahor. [11] He had the camels kneel down near the well outside the town; it was toward evening, the time the women go out to draw water.

[12] Then he prayed, "O LORD, God of my master Abraham, give me success today, and show kindness to my master Abraham. [13] See, I am standing beside this spring, and the daughters of the townspeople are coming out to draw

---

80 Matthew 6:33, RSV.

water. [14] *May it be that when I say to a girl, 'Please let down your jar that I may have a drink,' and she says, 'Drink, and I'll water your camels too'—let her be the one you have chosen for your servant Isaac. By this I will know that you have shown kindness to my master.''*

[15] *Before he had finished praying, Rebekah came out with her jar on her shoulder. She was the daughter of Bethuel son of Milcah, who was the wife of Abraham's brother Nahor.* [16] *The girl was very beautiful, a virgin; no man had ever lain with her. She went down to the spring, filled her jar and came up again.*

[17] *The servant hurried to meet her and said, "Please give me a little water from your jar.''*

[18] *"Drink, my lord," she said, and quickly lowered the jar to her hands and gave him a drink.*

[19] *After she had given him a drink, she said, "I'll draw water for your camels too, until they have finished drinking."* [20] *So she quickly emptied her jar into the trough, ran back to the well to draw more water, and drew enough for all his camels.* [21] *Without saying a word, the man watched her closely to learn whether or not the LORD had made his journey successful.*

❧

Now, even though the camels are a pretty significant feature in the story, I think we may consider them "optional equipment" in the package of guiding principles for seeking the proper wife. What you should notice is that the wife-seeker prays to God for the success of a strategy he has designed specifically to discern something I'll call "character."

Physical beauty is not *un*important, but it is readily apparent—and less important than character. Beauty is temporary; it can be taken away in an instant. It *will* fade away over time. But character is the greater treasure. A godly character is the firm foundation that will sustain a marriage regardless of the weight of sorrow or trial it must bear. Character endures the ravages of time and only grows stronger and more beautiful with the passage of years and the sharing of hopes and dreams and cares.

Take all the feminine loveliness you can find, gentlemen—if it is coupled with godly character. But flee beauty that lacks character.

On the other hand, do not be afraid to embrace character in whatever physical appearance you find it packaged, for character *becomes* beautiful in a person you love, prize, and nurture.

You should put yourself in places where women of godly character may be expected to go. And you should avoid places where godly women would not be expected to go. If you are not going to find women with the proper character in a certain place, or type of place, you are wasting your valuable time being there yourself. And you run the risk that you will become "entangled" with the women you *do* find there,[81] who do not meet the biblical standards for wives and can only complicate or derail your search.

You should shape your actions and your conversations so that a woman's character commitments are revealed. Look not so much for fashion sense or signs of popularity; look for the fruits of the Spirit[82] and an energy for "Kingdom business."[83]

Rebekah is a woman of godly character. We are told (or discover) that, in Rebekah, character consists of traits like responsibility, graciousness, generosity, respectfulness, humility, modesty, initiative, diligence, chastity, loyalty, and commitment.

∽◦⋞

The Bible says she is beautiful and a virgin. Sexual purity is desirable when searching for a wife—or a husband. There are a number of very practical benefits and no real drawbacks to sexual purity. But you aren't likely to find that kind of moral commitment among the Canaanites, or their modern-day equivalents.

---

[81] 2 Corinthians 6:14.
[82] Galatians 5:22-23.
[83] Ephesians 4:28.

The Bible is very clear and emphatic that some women are unsuitable from the start for consideration as potential wives for godly men—even though they are "readily available," so to speak.

It may seem bigoted and insensitive for a great religious role model like Abraham to exclude an entire group of women out of hand, but those who do not embrace the value system or acknowledge the sovereignty of his God are simply not qualified to be married to the man who will live out and perpetuate God's covenant promise.

Gentlemen, avoid women who are strangers to God or who live lives of rebellion against His Lordship.

❧

At this point, let me say a word to single women. Have I drawn the lines in such a way that you feel excluded, left standing on the outside looking in?

Perhaps you would like to be some Isaac's "Rebekah," but you're not a virgin. You want to be that woman of godly character, but you've had a child out of wedlock or gone through an ugly divorce. You may be wondering: "Does my past exclude me from consideration in some godly man's search for a proper bride?"

You cannot go back in time and make things different—that is true. What you have done in your life is done. But the more important question is: "What about now?" Have you repented and turned from sinful ways?

Godly character is built by training, but it is sustained by choice. You may have learned what character is the hard way, through your own painful mistakes. Even so, you may choose godly character now and become, with God's grace, that woman of character God created and intended you to be.

You can choose chastity today and every day, as a single woman through abstinence, or as a wife through fidelity. And do not settle for a man who lacks the integrity, honor, and character the Bible requires of a man who is to be a godly husband. God intends for godly single women to be somebody's Rebekah, and for godly single men to search for the women who properly meet their needs.

And what of those who have already established marriages, but didn't follow biblical principles in doing so?

There is grace here as well: God will bless any marriage—no matter how or why it got started—if and when the husband and wife submit themselves and their marriage to God's authority.

God can and will move any marriage in the right direction. But starting a marriage unbiblically—or behaving in a marriage in ways that are unbiblical—inevitably "sets you back" in regard to what God could and would have done in your marriage from the beginning, so that when you do finally give your marriage to God, you're making up lost ground.

Of course, making up lost ground is still a good site better than losing ground, which is what you do in the marriage not given over totally to God.

But the story goes on. Verse 50:

❧❦

⁵⁰ Laban and his household answered, "This is from the LORD; we can say nothing to you one way or the other. ⁵¹ Here is Rebekah; take her and go, and let her become the wife of your master's son, as the LORD has directed."
⁵² When Abraham's servant heard what they said, he bowed down to the ground before the LORD. ⁵³ Then the servant brought out gold and silver jewelry and articles of clothing and gave them to Rebekah; he also gave costly gifts to her brother and to her mother.

❧❦

When you take seriously your responsibility to seek a proper wife, you fulfill a significant family obligation to pass on to future generations the blessings of God' divine promise you're receiving. At the same time, if you would take a godly woman from *her* family to make her the partner in founding your own, you should give back to her family the best gifts you have to offer them. You should bless them and seek to enhance their family as well.

Now let's finish the story. Verse 61:

❧❧

⁶¹ Then Rebekah and her maids got ready and mounted their camels and went back with the man. So the servant took Rebekah and left.

⁶² Now Isaac had come from Beer Lahai Roi, for he was living in the Negev. ⁶³ He went out to the field one evening to meditate, and as he looked up, he saw camels approaching. ⁶⁴ Rebekah also looked up and saw Isaac. She got down from her camel ⁶⁵ and asked the servant, "Who is that man in the field coming to meet us?" "He is my master," the servant answered. So she took her veil and covered herself.

⁶⁶ Then the servant told Isaac all he had done. ⁶⁷ Isaac brought her into the tent of his mother Sarah, and he married Rebekah. So she became his wife, and he loved her; and Isaac was comforted after his mother's death.

❧❧

Even when the proper wife had been found—even when she consented to the marriage and came to the point of becoming his wife, the man was still a stranger to her, and *her* true identity was veiled from him. This is the way of marriage and you should expect it.

You enter into marriage with the person you have chosen—the person willing to be your lifetime partner—and each of you is still, in significant ways, a stranger to the other. Significant parts of who you are remain hidden, mysteries to be revealed over the course of time in the safety of a committed marriage.

❧❧

And let me point out that within "the Rebekah Project" there is generally a "Sarah Factor" to be dealt with. Isaac's mother, Sarah, had been the most significant woman in Isaac's life—until Rebekah came along. Isaac had the very good sense to move

Rebekah into Sarah's tent—to put his wife in the place of primacy in his life where his mother had been.

Isaac acquired a wife and his relationship with his mother (or in this case, with her memory) changed. You seek a godly wife and when you acquire her you are to place her in the central position in your earthly affections. You are to "forsake all others," whether their competition with your wife for your attention is sexual, emotional or psychological.

৶৽৽

The Rebekah Project was concluded when Isaac took Rebekah as his wife and loved her. Please notice the sequence: *"…she became his wife, and he loved her…."*

Maybe the biblical version of this particular project does not have a conclusion. While the search for the proper wife, guided and aided by God's unseen hand, achieves success and comes to an end, the love of that wife, made possible by God's love in us, is to continue as long as both lives shall last.

If you don't believe me, I encourage you young ladies and gentlemen to ask some of the Isaacs and Rebekahs in this place today. They know from experience—from many wonderful years of experience—that in this, as in everything, God's Word is ever true.

৶৽৽

Genesis 24 ESV

¹ Now Abraham was old, well advanced in years. And the Lord had blessed Abraham in all things. ² And Abraham said to his servant, the oldest of his household, who had charge of all that he had, "Put your hand under my thigh, ³ that I may make you swear by the Lord, the God of heaven and God of the earth, that you will not take a wife for my son from the daughters of the Canaanites, among whom I dwell, ⁴ but will go to my country and to my kindred, and take a wife for my son Isaac." ⁵ The servant said to him, "Perhaps the woman may not be willing to follow me to this land. Must I then take your son back to the land from which you came?" ⁶ Abraham said to him, "See to it that you do not take my son back there. ⁷ The Lord, the God of heaven, who took me from my father's house and from the land of my kindred, and who spoke to me and swore to me, 'To your offspring I will give this land,' he will send his angel before you, and you shall take a wife for my son from there. ⁸ But if the woman is not willing to follow you, then you will be free from this oath of mine; only you must not take my son back there." ⁹ So the servant put his hand under the thigh of Abraham his master and swore to him concerning this matter.

¹⁰ Then the servant took ten of his master's camels and departed, taking all sorts of choice gifts from his master; and he arose and went to Mesopotamia to the city of Nahor. ¹¹ And he made the camels kneel down outside the city by the well of water at the time of evening, the time when women go out to draw water. ¹² And he said, "O Lord, God of my master Abraham, please grant me success today and show steadfast love to my master Abraham. ¹³ Behold, I am standing by the spring of water, and the daughters of the men of the city are coming out to draw water. ¹⁴ Let the young woman to whom I shall say, 'Please let down your jar that I may drink,' and who shall say, 'Drink, and I will water your camels'—let her be the one whom you have appointed for your servant Isaac. By this I shall know that you have shown steadfast love to my master."

¹⁵ Before he had finished speaking, behold, Rebekah, who was born to Bethuel the son of Milcah, the wife of Nahor, Abraham's brother, came out with her water jar on her shoulder. ¹⁶ The young woman was very attractive in appearance, a maiden whom no man had known. She went down to the spring and filled her jar and came up. *17* Then the servant ran to meet her and said, "Please give me a little water to drink from your jar." *18* She said, "Drink, my lord." And she quickly let down her jar upon her hand and gave him a drink. *19* When she had finished giving him a drink, she said, "I will draw water for your camels also, until they have finished drinking." *20* So she quickly emptied her jar into the trough and ran again to the well to draw water, and she drew for all his camels. *21* The man gazed at her in silence to learn whether the Lord had prospered his journey or not.

22 When the camels had finished drinking, the man took a gold ring weighing a half shekel, and two bracelets for her arms weighing ten gold shekels, *23* and said, "Please tell me whose daughter you are. Is there room in your father's house for us to spend the night?" *24* She said to him, "I am the daughter of Bethuel the son of Milcah, whom she bore to Nahor." *25* She added, "We have plenty of both straw and fodder, and room to spend the night." *26* The man bowed his head and worshiped the Lord *27* and said, "Blessed be the Lord, the God of my master Abraham, who has not forsaken his steadfast love and his faithfulness toward my master. As for me, the Lord has led me in the way to the house of my master's kinsmen." *28* Then the young woman ran and told her mother's household about these things.

29 Rebekah had a brother whose name was Laban. Laban ran out toward the man, to the spring. *30* As soon as he saw the ring and the bracelets on his sister's arms, and heard the words of Rebekah his sister, "Thus the man spoke to me," he went to the man. And behold, he was standing by the camels at the spring.

31 He said, "Come in, O blessed of the Lord. Why do you stand outside? For I have prepared the house and a place for the camels."

32 So the man came to the house and unharnessed the camels, and gave straw and fodder to the camels, and there was water to wash his feet and the feet of the men who were with him. *33* Then food was set before him to eat. But he said, "I will not eat until I have said what I have to say." He said, "Speak on."

34 So he said, "I am Abraham's servant. *35* The Lord has greatly blessed my master, and he has become great. He has given him flocks and herds, silver and gold, male servants and female servants, camels and donkeys. [36] And Sarah my master's wife bore a son to my master when she was old, and to him he has given all that he has. [37] My master made me swear, saying, 'You shall not take a wife for my son from the daughters of the Canaanites, in whose land I dwell, [38] but you shall go to my father's house and to my clan and take a wife for my son.' [39] I said to my master, 'Perhaps the woman will not follow me.' [40] But he said to me, 'The Lord, before whom I have walked, will send his angel with you and prosper your way. You shall take a wife for my son from my clan and from my father's house. [41] Then you will be free from my oath, when you come to my clan. And if they will not give her to you, you will be free from my oath.'

[42] "I came today to the spring and said, 'O Lord, the God of my master Abraham, if now you are prospering the way that I go, [43] behold, I am standing by the spring of water. Let the virgin who comes out to draw water, to whom I shall say, "Please give me a little water from your jar to drink," [44] and who will say to me, "Drink, and I will draw for your camels also," let her be the woman whom the Lord has appointed for my master's son.'

[45] "Before I had finished speaking in my heart, behold, Rebekah came out with her water jar on her shoulder, and she went down to the spring and drew water. I said to her, 'Please let me drink.' [46] She quickly let down her jar from her shoulder and said, 'Drink, and I will give your camels drink also.' So I drank, and she gave the camels drink also. [47] Then I asked her, 'Whose daughter are you?' She said, 'The daughter of Bethuel, Nahor's son, whom Milcah bore to him.' So I put the ring on her nose and the bracelets on her arms. [48] Then I bowed my head and worshiped the Lord and blessed the Lord, the God of my master Abraham, who had led me by the right way to take the daughter of my master's kinsman for his son. [49] Now then, if you are going to show steadfast love and faithfulness to my master, tell me; and if not, tell me, that I may turn to the right hand or to the left."

[50] Then Laban and Bethuel answered and said, "The thing has come from the Lord; we cannot speak to you bad or good. [51] Behold, Rebekah is before you; take her and go, and let her be the wife of your master's son, as the Lord has spoken."

⁵² When Abraham's servant heard their words, he bowed himself to the earth before the Lord. ⁵³ And the servant brought out jewelry of silver and of gold, and garments, and gave them to Rebekah. He also gave to her brother and to her mother costly ornaments. ⁵⁴ And he and the men who were with him ate and drank, and they spent the night there. When they arose in the morning, he said, "Send me away to my master." ⁵⁵ Her brother and her mother said, "Let the young woman remain with us a while, at least ten days; after that she may go." ⁵⁶ But he said to them, "Do not delay me, since the Lord has prospered my way. Send me away that I may go to my master." ⁵⁷ They said, "Let us call the young woman and ask her." ⁵⁸ And they called Rebekah and said to her, "Will you go with this man?" She said, "I will go." ⁵⁹ So they sent away Rebekah their sister and her nurse, and Abraham's servant and his men. ⁶⁰ And they blessed Rebekah and said to her,

> *"Our sister, may you become thousands of ten thousands,*
> *and may your offspring possess the gate of those who hate him!"*

⁶¹ Then Rebekah and her young women arose and rode on the camels and followed the man. Thus the servant took Rebekah and went his way.

⁶² Now Isaac had returned from Beer-lahai-roi and was dwelling in the Negeb. ⁶³ And Isaac went out to meditate in the field toward evening. And he lifted up his eyes and saw, and behold, there were camels coming. ⁶⁴ And Rebekah lifted up her eyes, and when she saw Isaac, she dismounted from the camel ⁶⁵ and said to the servant, "Who is that man, walking in the field to meet us?" The servant said, "It is my master." So she took her veil and covered herself. ⁶⁶ And the servant told Isaac all the things that he had done. ⁶⁷ Then Isaac brought her into the tent of Sarah his mother and took Rebekah, and she became his wife, and he loved her. So Isaac was comforted after his mother's death.

৯৩৪৫

John 2:1-10 ESV

¹ On the third day there was a wedding at Cana in Galilee, and the mother of Jesus was there. ² Jesus also was invited to the wedding with his disciples. ³ When the wine ran out, the mother of Jesus said to him, "They have no wine." ⁴ And Jesus said to her, "Woman, what does this have to do with me? My hour has not yet come." ⁵ His mother said to the servants, "Do whatever he tells you."

⁶ Now there were six stone water jars there for the Jewish rites of purification, each holding twenty or thirty gallons. ⁷ Jesus said to the servants, "Fill the jars with water." And they filled them up to the brim. ⁸ And he said to them, "Now draw some out and take it to the master of the feast." So they took it. ⁹ When the master of the feast tasted the water now become wine, and did not know where it came from (though the servants who had drawn the water knew), the master of the feast called the bridegroom ¹⁰ and said to him, "Everyone serves the good wine first, and when people have drunk freely, then the poor wine. But you have kept the good wine until now."

৯৯৪৯

12.

Making a Good Marriage

Genesis 24; John 2:1-10 ESV

On the day after Christmas in 2004, the largest earthquake ever recorded created a tidal wave in the Indian Ocean that raced hundreds of miles in all directions and destroyed everything in its path. More than two hundred thousand people were killed. It was a disaster of biblical proportions.

The survivors have worked hard over the past decade to recover from the devastation and replace something of what they lost. They have a long way to go even now, just to get back to where they were. But before they could begin to rebuild, they had to confront the chaos and clear away the debris—which brings me to the parallel with today's sermon.

❧

A cultural and moral tsunami has rolled over our world in the past five decades or more—like successive waves of destruction, each washing away more of the vestiges of virtue and wholesome infrastructure in human society. One of the greatest casualties of this tectonic shift in the ground of human civilization has been the institution of marriage.

Changes in laws about divorce diminished society's support for maintaining marriage. And innovations in birth control technology spurred a tsunami of sexual activity on the part of individuals who were not married. The government legalized abortion, on the one hand, and provided an ongoing financial incentive, on the other, for creating children outside of marriage.

Personal preference has been enthroned as the supreme value in society and the promotion of time-tested moral norms related to marriage has been labeled "phobia" and "hate crime" in the secularization that has swept over the world.

And now, two generations into this tidal wave of moral transformation, marriage has been ripped from its moorings. And society—whose long-term strength and stability depends on marriage (though it doesn't think so)—is unraveling.

Recent research shows that men and women are getting married significantly later in their lives than their parents or their grandparents did, delaying for years the establishment of marriage-based families.[84] As disturbing as this growing trend is, it does not mean that families are not being established—just that more and more families are being formed outside the more nurturing environment of marriage.

On average, women in America are now more likely to have their first baby before they get married than after. Far more couples are "living together" before—or instead of—getting married—even though children born outside marriage are far more likely to have their parents split up than if their parents were married when they were conceived.

---

[84] Ezra Klein, "Nine facts about marriage and childbirth in the United States," *The Washington Post*, March 25, 2013, based on "Knot Yet: The Benefits and Costs of Delayed Marriage in America," a new report from the National Campaign to Prevent Teen and Unplanned Pregnancy, the National Marriage Project at the University of Virginia, and the RELATE Institute.

Marriage is now viewed in much of society as a final and optional step in a sexual relationship, rather than a mandatory first step—a "capstone" instead of a "cornerstone."

And many who have not yet married already expect to be married several times in their lives, as their circumstances and preferences change.

And sadly, in the case of young people, for whom decisions about marriage and family are still to be made, the attitudes and actions of marginal Christians as compared to non-Christians are not very different.[85]

Society is still celebrating these devastating changes and doing everything it can to keep the wave of social transformation riding high. But what we are observing is actually a disaster of biblical proportions that has broken upon us, with worse yet to come, as consequences accumulate. This is not the will of God as revealed in the Word of God.

As the world does all it can to destroy marriage, we as the Church—the Bride of Christ—must do all we can to rebuild marriage, even if the world resists us every step of the way. And before I tell you some of what the Bible tells us to do, let me clear away some of the debris that will make it harder for you to hear me.

⋙⋘

I know that many members of our church have been through failed marriages. Some were responsible, to a greater or lesser degree. Some were innocent victims of infidelity, abandonment or abuse. That's not what this sermon is about. What I have to say is not intended as a "guilt trip." I do not mean to hurt or condemn anyone here.

But at the same time, the discomfort an important truth causes us by reminding us of pain or guilt in our past must not prevent us

---

[85] The Barna Group, though these findings are challenged by others.

from saying what is true, if it needs to be said. Too much has been left unsaid for too long for that reason. You cannot correct what you will not confront.

And who better to raise a warning of danger than those who have already encountered that danger and suffered its destructive force?

And if what I have to say today does not apply to you, it will apply to someone you know—someone you love—someone who one day—if not now—will need to hear what God's Word has to say about how God wants us to handle His gracious gift of marriage. So if you don't need this sermon, pass it on to a child or grandchild or someone you know who does.

∿•∿

The Bible has much to say about marriage—more than we can say in one sermon. We have two stories today about the beginning of marriages. In Genesis, they are looking for a wife for Isaac, and in the Gospel of John, Mary looks to Jesus to fix a problem for a brand new bride and groom.

Both stories may seem, at first blush, a bit bizarre. Everybody but Isaac is enlisted in locating him a wife, and Jesus goes into the wine-making business so some wedding guests won't get sober at a reception.

But it's the Bible, so there must be some godly principles that are applicable, even for today.

For instance, believe it or not, for most of human history, everybody understood that the process of picking a marriage partner was too important and too risky—for the prospective bride and groom—*and* for their respective families—for the selection to be left up to the two people who were least qualified, by age and experience, to make a satisfactory choice. Today, the idea of "arranged marriages" seems as antiquated as the horse and buggy—or a camel caravan.

But consider the model the Bible presents.

In Genesis, Abraham—the leader of the family formed by God according to His divine and powerful promise—understands that the marriage of his son, Isaac, is about things a lot more important than the satisfaction of his son's sexual desires. Marriage is the key to a family's preservation and its prospects moving forward into the future. It is key to what the lives of those who get married will turn out to be. It is key to the possibilities that will be available to the children of that union.

For all these reasons, parents have a significant stake in the marriages of their children, and a moral responsibility to take an active role in the search for, and selection of, their children's life partner. Yet today, parents have been encouraged to abdicate that right and responsibility. Their children have been conditioned to believe that they alone should pick their partners—whether for marriage—or merely cohabitation—and that the selection should be based solely on the physical, emotional and psychological "rush" that the other person can provide—which is the popular definition of "love."

But Abraham sends his wisest and most trusted servant to search dispassionately for Isaac's wife.

And what are the criteria?

Abraham knows Isaac's wife needs to be from "their own people," even if this means somebody has to go to a lot of trouble to find her.

A person who is going to become part of your family—who will help form its identity in the years to come—must be "like" your family—an individual who shares your culture, your values, your faith and your perspective on life—or the family you have given your all to form will become a very different kind of family in the future, and all your efforts to provide a firm spiritual foundation for generations to come will have been wasted.

The servant prays that God will lead him to the right partner for Isaac. Parents should pray the same prayer and teach their children to pray it—long before they are aware they are searching.

The servant carefully considered what character and characteristics the proper marriage partner should have, and asked God to reveal those qualities. Children have to be raised by their parents with the qualities that make for a good husband or wife, if those qualities are to be there when it is time to become a marriage partner. And parents are much more likely to recognize those essential qualities—or their absence—in their children's potential partners because their wisdom and insight will be greater than their children's, who may find their own, more-limited discernment clouded by what they assume to be love.

⇛⇝

My experience over the past 35 years as a marriage counselor is that many marriages fail because one or both of the spouses are simply not capable of being an effective husband or wife.

They never learned how.

They were allowed to grow up self-focused and independent, believing they deserve whatever it is they want. No marriage can survive that mindset. As odd as it sounds, self-sacrifice and a servant spirit are the secrets to success and satisfaction in marriage. Raise your sons to be good husbands and your daughters to be good wives. There are far too few qualified candidates around today—male or female—and it shows.

Abraham ensured that the right person would be properly valued and richly rewarded.

We didn't read the whole story, which takes up all of the 24th Chapter of Genesis, but when Rebekah was revealed to be "the right one" and agreed to the marriage, she was showered with jewels. And she freely left the life she knew to enter into one that would be new to her.

Her family blessed her for her decision and supported her in it. And when she arrived in her new home and joined her new family, she was given "Sarah's tent," the place of the matriarch—the highest honor in the household.

And only after they were married does the Bible bother to mention that Isaac loved her. It turns out that the *desire* that *draws* individuals together is not the *love* that *holds* a marriage together.

Physical attraction, strong as it may be to begin with, may quickly and easily die. It is the love a husband and a wife *choose* to give one another after they are married that will sustain their marriage and secure their family against the hostility of a world weary of godly marriage.

Parents must not shirk their responsibility to help their children find and be good marriage partners—even when those marriages are many years in the future.

ॐ

And where does Jesus fit in? Look with me quickly at the lessons in John:

If you're going to get married, invite Jesus to come in and bless the marriage.

Know that a marriage without Jesus will soon be a sad and sobering affair.

Admit that you cannot do for your marriage—by yourself— what your marriage will need done.

Tell Jesus what the problems are.

Do whatever He tells you to do about them.

Recognize the miracles He does in and for the marriage.

Tell people how Jesus has made the marriage so much better than it could ever have been without Him.

ॐ

The flood overwhelming marriage these days is not God's doing. God makes marriages good, no matter what the world does. God makes good marriages, if you let Him.

And today, that is a miracle of biblical proportions!

ॐ

Genesis 25:21, 24-34; 27:1-10, 30-38 ESV

25 *²¹ And Isaac prayed to the Lord for his wife, because she was barren. And the Lord granted his prayer, and Rebekah his wife conceived.*

²⁴ When her days to give birth were completed, behold, there were twins in her womb. ²⁵ The first came out red, all his body like a hairy cloak, so they called his name Esau. ²⁶ Afterward his brother came out with his hand holding Esau's heel, so his name was called Jacob. Isaac was sixty years old when she bore them.

²⁷ When the boys grew up, Esau was a skillful hunter, a man of the field, while Jacob was a quiet man, dwelling in tents. ²⁸ Isaac loved Esau because he ate of his game, but Rebekah loved Jacob.

²⁹ Once when Jacob was cooking stew, Esau came in from the field, and he was exhausted. ³⁰ And Esau said to Jacob, "Let me eat some of that red stew, for I am exhausted!" (Therefore his name was called Edom) ³¹ Jacob said, "Sell me your birthright now." ³² Esau said, "I am about to die; of what use is a birthright to me?" ³³ Jacob said, "Swear to me now." So he swore to him and sold his birthright to Jacob. ³⁴ Then Jacob gave Esau bread and lentil stew, and he ate and drank and rose and went his way. Thus Esau despised his birthright.

27 ¹ When Isaac was old and his eyes were dim so that he could not see, he called Esau his older son and said to him, "My son," and he answered, "Here I am." ² He said, "Behold, I am old; I do not know the day of my death. ³ Now then, take your weapons, your quiver and your bow, and go out to the field and hunt game for me, ⁴ and prepare for me delicious food, such as I love, and bring it to me so that I may eat, that my soul may bless you before I die."

⁵ Now Rebekah was listening when Isaac spoke to his son Esau. So when Esau went to the field to hunt for game and bring it, ⁶ Rebekah said to her son Jacob, "I heard your father speak to your brother Esau, ⁷ 'Bring me game and prepare for me delicious food, that I may eat it and bless you before the Lord before I die.' ⁸ Now therefore, my son, obey my voice as I command you. ⁹ Go to the flock and bring me two good young goats, so that I may prepare from them delicious food for your father, such as he loves. *¹⁰ And you shall bring it to your father to eat, so that he may bless you before he dies."*

³⁰ As soon as Isaac had finished blessing Jacob, when Jacob had scarcely gone out from the presence of Isaac his father, Esau his brother came in from his hunting. ³¹ He also prepared delicious food and brought it to his father. And he said to his father, "Let my father arise and eat of his son's game, that you may bless me." ³² His father Isaac said to him, "Who are you?" He answered, "I am your son, your firstborn, Esau." ³³ Then Isaac trembled very violently and said, "Who was it then that hunted game and brought it to me, and I ate it all before you came, and I have blessed him? Yes, and he shall be blessed." ³⁴ As soon as Esau heard the words of his father, he cried out with an exceedingly great and bitter cry and said to his father, "Bless me, even me also, O my father!" ³⁵ But he said, "Your brother came deceitfully, and he has taken away your blessing." ³⁶ Esau said, "Is he not rightly named Jacob? For he has cheated me these two times. He took away my birthright, and behold, now he has taken away my blessing." Then he said, "Have you not reserved a blessing for me?" ³⁷ Isaac answered and said to Esau, "Behold, I have made him lord over you, and all his brothers I have given to him for servants, and with grain and wine I have sustained him. What then can I do for you, my son?" ³⁸ Esau said to his father, "Have you but one blessing, my father? Bless me, even me also, O my father." And Esau lifted up his voice and wept.

৵৹৻

Romans 9:6-16, 30-32 ESV

[6] *But it is not as though the word of God has failed. For not all who are descended from Israel belong to Israel,* [7] *and not all are children of Abraham because they are his offspring, but "Through Isaac shall your offspring be named."* [8] *This means that it is not the children of the flesh who are the children of God, but the children of the promise are counted as offspring.* [9] *For this is what the promise said: "About this time next year I will return, and Sarah shall have a son."* [10] *And not only so, but also when Rebekah had conceived children by one man, our forefather Isaac,* [11] *though they were not yet born and had done nothing either good or bad—in order that God's purpose of election might continue, not because of works but because of him who calls—* [12] *she was told, "The older will serve the younger."* [13] *As it is written, "Jacob I loved, but Esau I hated."*

[14] *What shall we say then? Is there injustice on God's part? By no means!* [15] *For he says to Moses, "I will have mercy on whom I have mercy, and I will have compassion on whom I have compassion."* [16] *So then it depends not on human will or exertion, but on God, who has mercy.*

[30] *What shall we say, then? That Gentiles who did not pursue righteousness have attained it, that is, a righteousness that is by faith;* [31] *but that Israel who pursued a law that would lead to righteousness did not succeed in reaching that law.* [32] *Why? Because they did not pursue it by faith, but as if it were based on works. They have stumbled over the stumbling stone.*

❧⋅❦

13.

Two Brothers—Two Meals

Genesis 25:21, 24-34 and 27:1-10, 30-38
Romans 9:6-16, 30-32 ESV

Late next month, the drama group here at the school[86] will take over this stage and begin rehearsing their spring play, *The Odd Couple*.[87] You may remember the movie or the television series. It's the story of two men of radically different personalities and perspectives who are forced to live together, with contentious and comic results.

There is an "Odd Couple" in the Bible—two men—two brothers—twins, actually (though hardly identical)—who are thrown together in a family where they spend they lives in conflict and competition as a result of radical differences in appearance, attitudes and agendas. Jacob and Esau—Esau and Jacob—

---

[86] For the first three years of its existence, one of the churches I pastored met for worship in the theatre of a private high school in town. Each Sunday morning, a crew of our people set up the stage as a church, complete with pulpit, lectern, altar table, choir chairs and a towering stained-glass window of the Resurrected Christ (on a slide projected on a huge retractable movie screen at the back of the stage). Each spring, we lost the use of this stage area for three weeks as the school drama class prepared for and presented its annual performance.

[87] Neil Simon, *The Odd Couple*, 1965.

wrestling even in the womb, will come out connected, not in brotherly love, but in a contest for supremacy that will center around birthrights and blessings and who will be the vehicle of God's promise in their generation.

Both, in their own way, are comic characters—the uncouth clod and the clever con man—and the episodes that unfold between them in the pages of the Bible would be hilarious if so much were not at stake for their family, their futures, and the fate of the world.

Neither is a particularly attractive person. Both have some pretty significant weaknesses. But you may find your attitudes about them shifting as the scenes in the story unfold. And you have to remember that there is another Actor—introduced at the beginning and intimately involved, but for now unseen—Whose part in the drama—or comedy—will eventually become clear.

༚⚬⚬

But the curtain goes up on our biblical Odd Couple as teenagers or young men.

Jacob is gathered around a camp fire, stirring a stew. He is a clean-cut fellow, calmly going about his domestic chore. In comes his brother—his *older* brother—if only by a few minutes.

Esau is sunburned, sweaty, hairy and hungry. His hunting gear is tossed aside with irritation because it hasn't done him any good today. Whatever Jacob has in the pot, Esau wants some of it—a lot of it!

And Jacob—cool, calm and collected—wants something Esau has.

"Jake! Gimme some of that…that…whatever it is!"

A brother should be generous. Whatever Jacob's got cooking in the pot—it didn't cost him anything. But Jacob is the younger brother—the second son in a culture where the firstborn gets everything—or nearly so: the family birthright and the father's

110

blessing. And so Jacob sees his chance to bargain for a better place than his birth order provided.

"I will give it to you—in trade—for your birthright," says Jacob, calmly stirring the pot. The birthright was the authority recognized by the community to take the place of the head of the household when the time came—to assume all the rights—and all the responsibilities—of the leader of the family, clan or tribe.[88] It was the firstborn son's by right—unless he chose to give it up. But what fool would do that? The birthright would be worth *everything* one day.

"Okay, but fill the bowl all the way up. I'm starving!"

And Jacob responds, "Let's make it official, shall we? Do you swear—on oath—before these witnesses—that you are voluntarily giving me your birthright in return for—what I am giving you?"

"I swear! Hurry up!"

And as calmly as he stirred the food, Jacob now calmly fills the bowl and hands it over to his rather unrefined brother.

Esau grabs the bowl, spills some of it on himself, and slurps down the rest.

"Hey, this isn't pot roast!"

"No, it's pea soup. But you can have all you want."

So Esau emptied the bowl and most of the pot, along with some bread and wine, got up and stomped off, leaving his birthright behind with the brother who was calmly—and cheerfully—cleaning up the mess.

Curtain—Act 1.

৵৹৶

The next time we see Esau, he is older. But some things haven't changed. He has the look—and smell—of someone who spends his days wandering through the wild places—more at home with animals—living and dead—than with people. He is a hunter still,

---

[88] O. J. Baab, "Birthright," *The Interpreter's Dictionary of the Bible*, Volume 1, George A. Buttrick, ed., New York, NY: Abingdon Press, 1962, pp.440-441.

thrilling to the kill. He is a man's man. He is his father's man—Isaac's first and favorite son.

Father Isaac is older, too. The years have made him rich—and blind. And Isaac, who learned as a child how precarious and unpredictable life can be,[89] has decided that it is time for the ritual meal in which he will pronounce the mystical blessing upon his son, speaking a future of power, prosperity and peace into existence for him. And so Isaac calls his Esau into his tent, and gives him instructions for the ritual feast.

But if Isaac's sight is gone, so, too, may be his hearing. For whatever reason, he has spoken loud enough for his wife, Rebekah, on the outside of the tent, to hear. And if the father of Esau and Jacob can pick a favorite son, so, too, can the woman who bore them.

As Esau leaves the stage in one direction, Jacob enters the scene from the other, and joins his mother who is hatching a plan to get him his father's blessing—or banishment from the family, if the plan backfires.

"Trust your Mamma," Rebekah tells him. "We'll get you that blessing."

So as Esau heads for the hills, Jacob heads for the herds. He's back in a flash with two young goats, and this time there *will* be a stew.

But the food is not the problem. It's Jacob. Rebekah's precious Jacob is "smooth." He is a smooth talker and a smooth dresser. He is also smooth-skinned. Even blind, Isaac will feel and smell the difference. And so Jacob must "become" his brother Esau in order to steal the latter's blessing.

৵৹৶

You gotta love watching persnickety Jacob strapping the hairy animal hides on his delicate hands and neck. You know he's gotta

---

[89] Genesis 22:1-13.

be thrilled to be slipping his body into Esau's never-been-washed—*never-been-fumigated*—hunting clothes. And just listen as he tries to turn his genteel voice into that rough and roaring brogue.

So here comes Jacob into Isaac's tent, dressed up like Bigfoot and carrying Momma's meal, ready to start the ceremony and pull the wool over his father's eyes—eyes that cannot see.

Even so, it's "touch and go" for a while. Isaac is old, but he hasn't lost *all* his senses. Jacob has to take the Lord's Name in vain, and betray his father and brother with a kiss, to pull it off. But after all—you do what you have to do to get what you want.

Jacob serves another meal—and walks away with his brother's blessing. And as soon as Jacob leaves the stage in one direction, Esau returns to the stage from the other.

The scene plays out again. The dialogue is the same, but it's all wrong. And what began as comedy is repeated as tragedy.

Esau did as he was told, but what's the point now?

Isaac has spoken the blessing and it can't be called back. And this time, Esau understands what it means: "O Father, bless me, too! Bless me, too!"

And all Isaac can say is, "I can bless you with nothing. Jacob is now the son of the Promise. His is the blessing *and* the birthright." But then Isaac adds, "But it will not always be so."

≈•≈

Two meals—and two brothers find their roles reversed. At the first meal, one brother cared too little. At the second, the other brother cared too much. Esau gave up his birthright and Jacob stole his blessing. Now the elder will serve the younger, just as the unseen Actor said, before the two brothers were born.

But now, even with blessing and birthright in his possession, clever, calculating, crooked Jacob cannot enjoy them. His schemes have shattered his family, and robbed him of the peace, prosperity and power he was promised. He must flee from his brother who now plans to kill him—and knows very well how to do it.

And the curtain closes as Jacob leaves the father he has deceived and a mother he will never see again.

If there were an intermission, it would come here. "*If*"—I said.

❧

To recap: Two brothers and two meals that changed everything.

But in time, the two brothers would become two families—then two nations—and finally two kinds of people. And the perspectives and agendas would remain the same. One kind of people wouldn't care enough about what that unseen Actor was doing, while the other kind of people would care too much and decide it was up to them to make sure they were the ones who got what that Actor was giving—the special promise of divine blessing.

And finally, a time came when, to the sheer amazement of those who had gone to such great lengths to ensure that they always possessed the birthright and the blessing, the roles switched again. Those who had been left out for so long received the blessing—through no effort or merit of their own—and those who had enjoyed the birthright for so long suddenly found themselves without it. So says the Apostle Paul in Romans, Chapter 3.[90]

Jacob and the people like him didn't realize that the eternal blessing—the redemption, the grace, the hope of glory—was something that the unseen Actor—God—gave to whoever He wanted to give it. It was not something you could wheel-and-deal and deceive for.

And the people like Esau discovered one day that even if you lost your right—even if you *threw away* your right—to God's blessing, if you were willing to receive it, God would give it back

---

[90] Romans 3:21-31.

to you. You can have the blessing if you will accept it as a gift from God.

৯৯৯

The intermission is over. Time for the final act of this biblical play. The curtain is going up on one more meal.

The setting is centuries after the time of Jacob and Esau. The scene is an upper room in Jerusalem. The table is set once again for a ritual meal. There are now, not two brothers, but twelve. One is there with treachery in mind, but the Master of the meal is not deceived, and will pronounce God's blessings properly on those who have received the birthright of salvation in the only way they can—by faith.

As in Genesis, there is bread and wine, but here the bread becomes something sacramental in the hands of the One Who blesses it, breaks it, and calls it His Body. The wine He shares with them becomes the symbol of a sacrifice in blood even greater than the one Isaac avoided.[91]

In the first meal, Esau traded his birthright for a mess of pottage. At this meal, his spiritual descendants trade their sins for a birthright as God's children.

In the second meal, Jacob thought he had to steal a blessing that, in reality, God was going to give him, no matter what he did.

In this third meal, the Son of God gathers Jacob's descendants and shows them that God blesses all who come in faith to receive what no one can take from Him—by trick or trade.

Someone once said, "The play's the thing!"[92] There's none better than this one, and you are all invited to join the cast. In a moment, rehearsals will begin—around the Lord's Table.

৯৯৯

---

[91] Genesis 22:1-13.
[92] William Shakespeare, *Hamlet*, Act 2, Scene 2, Line 604, c.1599.

Genesis 32:22-31 RSV

[22] *The same night [Jacob] arose and took his two wives, his two maids, and his eleven children, and crossed the ford of the Jabbok.* [23] *He took them and sent them across the stream, and likewise everything that he had.* [24] *And Jacob was left alone; and a man wrestled with him until the breaking of the day.* [25] *When the man saw that he did not prevail against Jacob, he touched the hollow of his thigh; and Jacob's thigh was put out of joint as he wrestled with him.* [26] *Then he said, "Let me go, for the day is breaking." But Jacob said, "I will not let you go, unless you bless me."* [27] *And he said to him, "What is your name?" And he said, "Jacob."* [28] *Then he said, "Your name shall no more be called Jacob, but Israel, for you have striven with God and with men, and have prevailed."* [29] *Then Jacob asked him, "Tell me, I pray, your name." But he said, "Why is it that you ask my name?" And there he blessed him.* [30] *So Jacob called the name of the place Peni'el, saying, "For I have seen God face to face, and yet my life is preserved."* [31] *The sun rose upon him as he passed Penu'el, limping because of his thigh.* [32] *Therefore to this day the Israelites do not eat the sinew of the hip which is upon the hollow of the thigh, because he touched the hollow of Jacob's thigh on the sinew of the hip.*

৵৽৶

14.

The God Who Goes "Bump" in the Night

Genesis 32:22-31 RSV

Have you noticed?

In neighborhoods around the area, decorations are popping up. Creepy figures dot the lawns and pumpkins everywhere are poised to put on frightful grins. Halloween is coming, and with it our plans to embrace (or avoid) the traditions that focus on "dangerous forces lurking in the dark." It is, perhaps, an appropriate time to offer up that traditional Scottish prayer that says,

> "From ghoulies and ghosties
> And long-leggedy beasties
> And things that go bump in the night,
> Good Lord, deliver us!"[93]

୮୮

But suppose the good Lord *is* the Thing that goes "bump" in the night. What do you do when the dangerous force lurking in the darkness is not demonic, but divine?

Let's find out.

---

[93] James Hardy, ed., *The Denham Tracts*, London: Folklore Society, 1895, vol. 2, pp. 76-80.

We just heard a scary story found in Genesis, Chapter 32. The Patriarch Jacob is settling in for the night on the supposedly safe side of the Jabbok, a river that borders the Promised Land.

If we had read from the beginning of the chapter, you would have seen why the other side of the river wouldn't seem too safe for Jacob.

Jacob wants to come home. He's been gone a very long time.

But there's a problem. Jacob has a brother who may not be too happy to see him—a brother who may not let him come home—a brother who may not let him *live*.

Do you remember the story?

Many years before, Jacob asked his father for a blessing he didn't deserve, and then ran away from home when he got it. He was not a prodigal son,[94] though he was a deceptive one. He did not lose his father's property "living high," or sink to feeding pigs to "pick up" his lunch. Jacob went to stay with relatives and, over the years, made a small fortune in the livestock business. He "married up" (as they say) and became the head of a large and growing family.

But Jacob wants to go home. His father is long dead, but the older brother Jacob cheated is still there, and may not be any happier to see him come down the road than the older brother in the prodigal son parable had been. So Jacob, the middle-aged patriarch, forms a plan, just as the young prodigal did in the parable Jesus told.

Both plans involve a show of public humility, but Jacob is able to throw in a lot more material resources to sweeten the deal.

Still, he worries about what his brother will do. He sends messengers to his brother. They return to say his brother is coming out to meet him—with a small army of men behind him.

As we pick up the story, Jacob has set in motion—literally—his plan for dealing with his brother.

---

[94] Luke 15:11-32.

But before he sees his brother, Jacob will have a little unexpected business to attend to.

Jacob will have to wrestle with God.

෨๛

Jacob had not intended to wrestle with God. God had been good to Jacob and had even shown a special interest in him from time to time.

Jacob had had some close encounters with God,[95] but most of the time, Jacob was focused on his family, his business, his life. He had enough to do just getting through each day, with its hardships and hazards, without looking for God behind every pile of rocks or in every shifting shadow of the night. Jacob wasn't looking for a wrestling match with God.

But God had other plans. You see, Jacob was there at the Jabbok because God had led him there.

Jacob had dreamed of God, many years before, and called the place where he dreamed, "Bethel"—which is Hebrew for "the House of God." But at "Peniel"—the place he will call "the Face of God," Jacob will come to know God in a very different way. There will be no sleeping in the darkness at Peniel. Here, Jacob will find himself locked in an encounter with God that is "up close and personal."

Sometimes the most difficult struggles in life are the ones you have with God, though it may take you awhile to realize that it's God Who's got a hold of you. Jacob does not know the name and cannot see the face of his Attacker. All he knows is that Someone has grabbed him and that he is alone in his struggle with his Adversary.

While Jacob is obsessed with fear that his brother will attack him—while Jacob is exhausted from all his meticulous preparations for his long-awaited homecoming—while Jacob is all

---

[95] Genesis 28:10-17; 31:1-5.

alone in a strange place on a dark night—God pounces. And the wrestling match Jacob doesn't want—and hasn't asked for—begins.

No matter how meticulous your planning and how great your effort to control your life and its outcomes, God can break in at any time and wrestle control of it away from you. God breaks into life and changes plans.

But Jacob does remarkably well. Though taken off guard, Jacob holds on and struggles on. Hour after hour throughout the long night, Jacob wrestles with this powerful and dangerous Stranger. More than once in his life, Jacob has turned his superior strength to his advantage.[96] But on this night, with *this* Adversary, there is only enough power in Jacob's body to avoid defeat; there is not enough to bring him victory. The Stranger will not be overcome by physical force.

But Jacob also has a quick and resourceful mind. Perhaps the advantage that eludes his hands can be won through his words. There are, after all, different ways of wrestling with someone.

Jacob refuses to end the struggle without some benefit for the effort—and the suffering.

The Stranger senses the approach of dawn and the return of the light. "Let's call it a draw," He says.

Understand: The danger in daybreak is related to Jacob, not to God. God will tell Moses in Exodus 33, *"...you cannot see my face, for no one may see me and live."*[97]

God struggles with Jacob. God strikes Jacob in a way that will forever change Jacob's life. But God wants Jacob alive for what God has in mind for him.

Jacob, for his part, is willing to risk his life—for the opportunity to benefit from this costly encounter. "Bless me!" he says. Where most would have seen only the danger, Jacob sees possibility. Something good could come out of this experience: "I

---

[96] Genesis 28:11; 29:10.
[97] Exodus 33:20, RSV.

will not let You go unless You bless me. I'm going to hold on to You, no matter what!"

But God ignores Jacob's call for a blessing until they have dealt with *God's* agenda: the business of Jacob's identity—the true nature of the man expressed in his name.

"What is your name? Admit who you really are!"

જ્જઓ

And with that, for Jacob, whose name does indicate his nature, the contest is over. Jacob cannot win this encounter with brute force or clever repartee. And now he cannot hope to receive the blessing he wants—unless he owns up to his deceitful ways and confesses his true nature.

Jacob has to own up to his true identity—so that God can give him a new one. "I am Jacob, the supplanter, the one always trying to take something from someone else." But from this mysterious Stranger, Jacob can take nothing. He can *take* nothing—but he can *receive* everything!

God attacks the person Jacob is—and defeats him. It is Jacob who is attacked, but when the battle is done, it is Israel who survives.

"You may have been Jacob, the sneaky, crafty manipulator, but you will be Israel, who strives with God and for whom God will strive."

In the struggle between Jacob and God, God lays His hand on Jacob and makes him what God wants (and needs) him to be, in order for God to tie the divine plan for the human race and all Creation to this particular man.

"You have survived so far; you have prevailed. Now, My blessing—My promise—is that I will see that you continue to do so."

To see God, even in the shadows of the night, is not to be unchanged—unscathed. God marks him, renames him, and blesses him. Jacob is "marked" for success—marked by his struggle with God.

Jacob lives a new way, with a new power—and a new weakness. Jacob is broken—and reborn.

God says that Jacob has prevailed. Jacob says only that he has survived. Jacob starts down the road of the truly victorious life when he recognizes the supremacy of God over it. The ultimate test: Does God's favor mean more than life itself?

Jacob has come face to face with his God. Now he is ready to come face to face with his brother—the brother he so frequently wronged. With the ending of the night and his struggle with God, Jacob goes in the light of morning to meet his brother. But he goes not as Jacob; he goes as Israel.

Israel, as a person and a later as a nation, will always be at risk from his neighbors, but it is God Who poses the greatest threat, and God Who provides the greatest protection. The Bible records that Israel will always be struggling with God—wrestling with God—especially when the people called Israel have isolated themselves in moral and spiritual darkness.

&⸺⸻

And what about us?

There is a good deal of "Jacob" in all of us, really: just trying to get ahead—willing to take a short cut once in a while, if we can get away with it—willing to take advantage of others, if they're not paying attention.

But we don't always get away with it—and taking advantage of others can leave us, eventually, all alone and far from anywhere we would call our "heart's home."

There's a bit of the Jacob in all of us. As with Jacob, God comes in that dark and unexpected moment, and wrestles with us.

And when you find that the One you're wrestling with is God, the first thing to do is hold on tight. Then you want to try to find out more about Him. And finally, you had better "stand by," because sooner or later, His power will be revealed in you.

When that mysterious presence and power that you cannot escape and cannot defeat and cannot control comes upon you, hold on for dear life—and eternal life—and confess who you are, knowing that, in all the pain and confusion and danger, there is a life-changing blessing—and a life-blessing change—in the balance.

When God comes upon us, we are "Jacobs." But God comes upon us to make us like Israel—one who has struggled with God and man, and prevailed. If you have wrestled with God and survived, you can handle anything the world can throw your way. Jacob was afraid of his brother when the sun went down. He was afraid of no man when the dawn revealed a new and different day. He came to the Jabbok as Jacob; he crossed it as Israel.

৵৽৽ঌ

This dark night spent wrestling with God also has its New Testament parallel: The disciples fell asleep in Gethsemane,[98] like Jacob did at Bethel.[99] But like Jacob at the Jabbok, Jesus was wide awake in the Garden and wrestling alone with God throughout that night, wrestling with God over the costly will of God for His life. Jesus saw what Jacob was denied: Jesus saw His Heavenly Father face to face. And Jesus knew and spoke the Name that Jacob was not told: *"Abba Father."*[100]

Jesus strove with God and with the desires of His own human heart in the Garden of Gethsemane—and He prevailed as the faithful Son and Suffering Servant of God.

Jacob wrestled with God alone in the darkness, and he became Israel, the broken founder of a sacred nation. Jesus struggled with God that night in Gethsemane, and as He humbled Himself,[101]

---

[98] Matthew 26:36-45.
[99] Genesis 28:10-19.
[100] Mark 14:36.
[101] Philippians 2:8.

God confirmed Him as the Christ He was born into this world to be.[102] God made Jesus, in His weakness, the Pioneer of our faith[103] and the first fruits of the Resurrection of the dead.[104]

The nation of Israel was born of Jacob's body, children of the one who wrestled in that dark place with God and prevailed. And now we are reborn in the Body of Christ, preserved alive in Him for all eternity as the children—and the New Israel—of God.[105]

Whoever you are—whatever your name, whatever your nature—however far from home you have run or strayed—and however dark your life—Jesus stands ready to give you a new nature and a new name—His nature[106] and His name.[107] Give up the struggle and accept God's grace. Jesus is the Light no darkness can penetrate.[108] Today can be the glorious day of your salvation.[109] Blest and broken, cross over the river and come home to the Promised Land God has prepared for you.[110]

಄

---

[102] John 3:16-17.
[103] Hebrews 12:2.
[104] 1 Corinthians 15:20.
[105] 1 Peter 1:23.
[106] 2 Peter 1:4.
[107] Revelation 3:12.
[108] John 1:4-5.
[109] 2 Corinthians 6:2.
[110] John 14:2-3.

15.

The Secret of Survival

Genesis 37-50 RSV

The little boy was curious when the preacher took his wristwatch off and placed it on the pulpit—as I am now doing with mine. "What does it mean when the preacher does that, Daddy?" The father replied sadly, "Not a thing, Son, not a thing."

Time will tell, of course, if the same gesture will mean anything today.

I draw your attention to my watch for a reason: It's a TIMEX. Years ago, you could watch many of its cousins being smashed and bashed and abused on TV. And after each ordeal, the announcer would hold the poor thing up to the camera, proclaiming proudly: "TIMEX...takes a licking and keeps on ticking!"[111]

Can you empathize with the TIMEX? Some people know better than others what it's like to take a licking. Some of you in this room took a licking this week—at work—in school—maybe even at home. Some of you have taken quite a few lickings over the years.

---

[111] The announcer was newsman John Cameron Swayze, and the commercials ran from 1956 to 1976.

So maybe it's worth our time to ask the question: "How is it that some people can take a licking and keep on ticking, while others—are just licked?"

Suppose, for instance, you're 17 years old and your father's pride and joy. You've got a super wardrobe and lots of self-confidence and dreams of great things to come. Then one day you lose *everything.*

Are you licked, or do you keep on ticking?

Suppose you work like a slave, and after a while, earn your boss's trust. You begin to see some slight glimmer of hope for a future in the organization. Then somebody you haven't done anything to destroys your reputation, accusing you of some unethical behavior you have taken extreme measures to avoid. You lose your job—and your benefits. You get punished—even though you're innocent!

Still ticking? Or are you licked?

Suppose you start over *again* and build up a little seniority. You get some responsibility, but you just can't find the key to get yourself out of the dead-end situation you're locked into. You go out of your way to help people get back on *their* feet (where they could do the same for you), and they forget you like you never happened.

How can you keep on ticking when your life seems like one continuous licking? How can you hold on to a faith that will sustain you in a world filled with people more than happy to hurt you? How does Joseph, the son of Jacob, do it?

శ్రం

We don't have time to read the 13 chapters in Genesis that tell Joseph's story, but we do have time to look for the secret of his survival. The story begins in Genesis 37 with a teenager hated by his brothers and loved by his father.

You'd think families could get along, but they don't, most of them, and this one is no exception. It's not a perfect family, and

Joseph's not perfect, either. But God has something to tell us here, so let's see if we can find it.

This beloved and despised young fellow has some dreams.[112] They're weird dreams; but they're cool dreams, too (from his perspective). Joseph dreams about wheat growing up and stars shining down. And somehow, he knows that the dreams are about him. To him, the dreams are saying, "Joseph rules!"

So he says to his family, "I'm Number One! I'm Number One!"

And you know, his brothers don't like him any better than they did before.

But Jacob, his father, just watches and wonders. You see, Jacob is the "last who became first."[113] Jacob is the one who dreamed of angels climbing up and down a ladder between heaven and earth at a spot he called Bethel[114]—and of a God making promises about a *special place*, and a *chosen people*, and a *sacred purpose*, and a *divine Presence*. Jacob is a child of the Promise like his father, Isaac, before him. And he knows that one of *his* sons will be the child of the Promise, and God-only-knows which one it will be. But sometimes dreams are from God and Joseph's dreams sound an awful lot like the Promise.[115]

How much of this Joseph understands, we don't know. How much Jacob told his sons, we don't know. We do know that Joseph is a kid with a dream. And when he loses everything else,[116] it is the dream—and the Promise contained in it—that keep him ticking. He remembers the dream God has given him, a dream about "What Will Be." And he trusts the Promise in the dream, and the God who made it, which redefines the meaning of "What Is."

---

112 Genesis 37:5-11.
113 Genesis 25:21-26.
114 Genesis 28:10-17.
115 Genesis 12:2-3.
116 Genesis 37:18-28.

So the difference between defeat and survival is, first of all, the possession of a dream—or a vision, or an insight, or an awareness—a revelation of some kind—that God's eternal promise has been given to you—that *you* are a child of the promise—that what God promises you is *The* Promise:

- a special *place*
  (as in, *"I go to prepare a place for you..."*[117])
- and a special *identity*
  (as in, *"...that we should be called the children of God"*[118])
- and a special *purpose*
  (as in, *"Ye shall be my witnesses..."*[119])
- and a special *Presence*
  (as in, *"Lo, I am with you always..."*[120]).

When you know that this is "What Will Be" for you, then "What Is" for you at any given moment, or *every* given moment, becomes a part of the fulfillment of the Promise. We seldom understand how the events or experiences of any given moment fit into "What Will Be." But that God *is* fitting them in is the secret assurance that sustains us.

☙❧

So Joseph is stripped of his beautiful coat, his freedom, and his place in the family. He's stripped of his innocence and youthful cockiness in the bargain. He's stripped of any possibility of living the life that would have been his. He's left a slave—in a stranger's house—in a foreign land. But he has the memory of a special dream locked safely in his heart.

Oh, and God is with him.

---

[117] John 14:3, RSV.
[118] 1 John 3:1, RSV.
[119] Acts 1:8, RSV.
[120] Matthew 28:20, RSV.

It's almost laughable. But the Bible says: *"The Lord was with Joseph."*[121]

"Well, he's got a funny way of showing it!"

Our ideas about what constitutes "God-with-us" don't often include slavery—and poverty—and danger—and fear.

How can you say that God is with anybody in conditions like these?

Well, shall we quote "...one set of footprints in the sand"?[122]

Or perhaps:

> *"Yea, though I walk*
> *through the valley of the shadow of death,*
> *I will fear no evil,*
> **for thou art with me.**"[123]

How do you know if—or when—God is with you?

It's easy enough to believe in the presence of a God Who comes healing the sick[124] or walking on water.[125] But just as often, God-with-us is like a face unseen and a voice unheard. God is with us in ways we cannot understand. But we can know that God is with us because it is part of the Promise, and we are children of the Promise, just like Joseph.

Joseph *knows* that God is with him. He has *no* doubt. And in his adversity, Joseph prospers.[126] God is *so* with him that Joseph even causes his captors and tormentors to prosper, in spite of the adversity. Through more than a dozen years of this adversity[127]— through one injustice after another[128]—Joseph works and trusts and waits. And that's okay, because he still has the dream God gave him, and he knows that God is with him (and showing him

---

121 Genesis 39:2, RSV.
122 Poem "Footprints in the Sand," Mary Stevenson, 1936.
123 Psalm 23:4, KJV.
124 Mark 1:34.
125 Matthew 4:25.
126 Genesis 39:2-6.
127 Genesis 37:2; 41:46.
128 Genesis 39:7-21; 40:20-23.

steadfast love, by the way) because that's part of God's Promise. That's part of God's promise to Joseph, and part of God's promise to every child who claims the Promise.

ॐ∙ॐ

And then one day, God fulfills the dream: Joseph rules.[129] Joseph rules Egypt. He rules it under Pharaoh, officially. But since Joseph knows what to do and Pharaoh doesn't, Joseph really rules Pharaoh, too. And since everybody outside Egypt, including his brothers, has to come *to* Egypt to eat (or die), Joseph rules them, too.[130]

But waiting for the dream's fulfillment and feeling the fellowship of God through years of adversity has taught Joseph a very important truth: No matter how great his rule, Joseph will never be "Number One." God is "Number One" and Joseph is a distant second under God. God gives dreams and God provides the interpretation of these dreams.[131] God promises to be with us—and He is present with us—for a purpose.

The point of the servitude and injustice was not to make Joseph miserable. The point of the prestige and power is not to raise Joseph's morale. The Promise is also about purpose—God's purpose—God's purpose in creating us and sharing each day of our lives with us. Without that purpose, Joseph's prosperity is like winning the lottery: It's a meaningless fluke. The purpose of *everything* that happens to Joseph—from God's perspective—is the preservation of life.[132]

So the story is not over when Joseph makes it to the top. Yes, life gets a lot better for him; it's completely transformed.[133] No conversion could be more dramatic, at least in human terms. It

---

[129] Genesis 41:39-44.
[130] Genesis 42:1-17.
[131] Genesis 41:16.
[132] Genesis 45:7.
[133] Genesis 41:45.

looks as though he goes from "nothing" to "everything." He has a family and makes his sons a living testimony that God has wiped the hardships from his memory and made him fruitful far from home.[134]

But Joseph's adversity continues in the midst of prosperity because he is still far from home and cut off from the family he longs to see. To possess high position and great power can be very painful if they cannot provide you what you want and need most.

Now Joseph didn't realize this when his brothers threw him down the well in Dothan.[135] He didn't have this in mind when he was sold to Potiphar[136] or went "streaking" away from Mrs. Potiphar's lust.[137] There's no indication Joseph spent his time in prison explaining to the other inmates what God had in mind for his life.[138] It isn't until his faithful trust in God through all these dark days has prepared him for the life-saving mission he's given that he is able to look at the whole experience and say, "*This* is what God sent me here to do."[139]

છ⊸છ

The Promise of God requires faith on our part because we don't normally see the fulfillment in advance. It doesn't become clear until we get there. Every day Joseph wakes up in adversity is a day he has to answer the question, "Do I still believe the Promise?"

And every day, he is able to tell himself, "I believe the Promise of God, and I trust in the presence of God, so I must be a part of the purpose of God."

And he survives.

---

[134] Genesis 41:50-52.
[135] Genesis 37:22-24.
[136] Genesis 39:1.
[137] Genesis 39:11-12.
[138] Genesis 39:20.
[139] Genesis 45:4-8.

So how far do you trust God? Can you be content knowing your very existence is part of God's grand purpose and design? Are you willing to give your life to God to be used according to His purpose? Are you willing to let God decide what your life will be—to let God set the agenda without submitting a copy for your approval each day?

Hard questions, but we need to ask them.

Joseph seems to believe that God is actively involved in every aspect of his life. And rightly so.

The power of God's *promise* preserves Joseph when he loses everything.

The power of God's *presence* sustains Joseph through years of hardship and disappointment.

The power of God's *purpose* protects Joseph from the temptations of overwhelming affluence when the tables are turned in his favor.

❦

But there is more, for Joseph finally comes to understand that in addition to being God's person, he is also a part of God's people, and that God has truly prepared a place for him among them.

The power of God's *providence* enables Joseph to forgive the brothers who betrayed him and return to the father who thought him dead.

And how is it that Joseph can be satisfied to lift the sweet cup of reconciliation to their lips when he has the power to pour the bitter cup of revenge down their throats?

Joseph has now come to recognize the final key: They meant it for evil, *"but God meant it for good."*[140]

His brothers meant all they did to him for evil, but God took what they did and transformed it, according to His eternal plan, into their salvation. Potiphar's wife meant her lust and lies against

---

[140] Genesis 50:15-20, RSV.

him for evil, but God took what she did and transformed it, according to His eternal plan, so that she and her household and all the people *"might have life, and have it more abundantly."*[141]

The truth is that all of us can play the part of Joseph to one degree or another. Every one of us has experienced evil at the hand of this person or that. And every one of us has discovered that God meant it for good. God took the evil we encountered and turned it inside out and blessed us in the midst of, or in spite of, or because of, what we thought was simply somebody's evil attack. Somehow, it fit into a marvelous, mysterious, God-guided plan.

For that, we should raise our voices in praise and open our hearts in forgiveness that models the greater forgiveness of God.[142] Our suffering is as nothing compared to the wonder of our adoption and the grandeur of our inheritance as children of the Promise.[143]

But the truth is also that we can play the part of Joseph's brothers and the others guilty of evil. And we mean at least some of what we say and do and think for evil, too. But God also means *our* evil for good, and He takes what we have said and done and thought, and washes the stain of sin out of it, and gives it back to us clean and bright and good.[144]

৯৯⋲৯

And for that we should fall on our faces in repentance[145]—and gratitude[146]—for the promise is still available to us,[147] and His Presence is still present with us,[148] and that heavenly home is still

---

[141] John 10:10, RSV.
[142] Matthew 6:9-13.
[143] Romans 8:18.
[144] Isaiah 1:18; 1 John 1:9.
[145] Luke 18:13.
[146] Luke 17:11-16.
[147] Acts 2:39.
[148] Matthew 28:20.

prepared for us,[149] because one day a Father sent His best loved Son to look for the others who had wandered far from home.[150] And though they attacked Him, and the Son was thought to be dead, He was raised in power and glory to save all who called upon His Name.[151]

It was good news for both Joseph *and* his brothers, and it is good news for us: *"...in everything God works for good with those who love him, who are called according to his purpose."*[152]

So you are a survivor. You're still "ticking," despite what you've been through.

And now you know why:

God's promise—

God's presence—

God's purpose—

God's providence.

Don't keep the secret of your survival a secret.

∾∿

---

[149] John 14:3.

[150] Luke 19:10.

[151] Acts 22:14-16.

[152] Romans 8:28, RSV.

Genesis 39 ESV

¹ Now Joseph had been brought down to Egypt, and Potiphar, an officer of Pharaoh, the captain of the guard, an Egyptian, had bought him from the Ishmaelites who had brought him down there. ² The Lord was with Joseph, and he became a successful man, and he was in the house of his Egyptian master. ³ His master saw that the Lord was with him and that the Lord caused all that he did to succeed in his hands. ⁴ So Joseph found favor in his sight and attended him, and he made him overseer of his house and put him in charge of all that he had. ⁵ From the time that he made him overseer in his house and over all that he had, the Lord blessed the Egyptian's house for Joseph's sake; the blessing of the Lord was on all that he had, in house and field. ⁶ So he left all that he had in Joseph's charge, and because of him he had no concern about anything but the food he ate.

Now Joseph was handsome in form and appearance. ⁷ And after a time his master's wife cast her eyes on Joseph and said, "Lie with me." ⁸ But he refused and said to his master's wife, "Behold, because of me my master has no concern about anything in the house, and he has put everything that he has in my charge. ⁹ He is not greater in this house than I am, nor has he kept back anything from me except you, because you are his wife. How then can I do this great wickedness and sin against God?" ¹⁰ And as she spoke to Joseph day after day, he would not listen to her, to lie beside her or to be with her.

¹¹ But one day, when he went into the house to do his work and none of the men of the house was there in the house, ¹² she caught him by his garment, saying, "Lie with me." But he left his garment in her hand and fled and got out of the house. ¹³ And as soon as she saw that he had left his garment in her hand and had fled out of the house, ¹⁴ she called to the men of her household and said to them, "See, he has brought among us a Hebrew to laugh at us. He came in to me to lie with me, and I cried out with a loud voice. ¹⁵ And as soon as he heard that I lifted up my voice and cried out, he left his garment beside me and fled and got out of the house." ¹⁶ Then she laid up his garment by her until his master came home, ¹⁷ and she told him the same story, saying, "The Hebrew servant, whom you have brought among us, came in to me to laugh at me. [18] But as soon as I lifted up my voice and cried, he left his garment beside me and fled out of the house."

[19] As soon as his master heard the words that his wife spoke to him, "This is the way your servant treated me," his anger was kindled. [20] And Joseph's master took him and put him into the prison, the place where the king's prisoners were confined, and he was there in prison. [21] But the Lord was with Joseph and showed him steadfast love and gave him favor in the sight of the keeper of the prison. [22] And the keeper of the prison put Joseph in charge of all the prisoners who were in the prison. Whatever was done there, he was the one who did it. [23] The keeper of the prison paid no attention to anything that was in Joseph's charge, because the Lord was with him. And whatever he did, the Lord made it succeed.

తళ్ళ

Matthew 4:1-11 ESV

¹ Then Jesus was led up by the Spirit into the wilderness to be tempted by the devil. ² And after fasting forty days and forty nights, he was hungry. ³ And the tempter came and said to him, "If you are the Son of God, command these stones to become loaves of bread." ⁴ But he answered, "It is written,

> *Man shall not live by bread alone,*
> > *but by every word*
> > *that comes from the mouth of God.""*

⁵ Then the devil took him to the holy city and set him on the pinnacle of the temple ⁶ and said to him, "If you are the Son of God, throw yourself down, for it is written,

> *He will command his angels concerning you,'*

and

> *On their hands they will bear you up,*
> > *lest you strike your foot against a stone.""*

⁷ Jesus said to him, "Again it is written,

> *You shall not put the Lord your God to the test.""*

⁸ Again, the devil took him to a very high mountain and showed him all the kingdoms of the world and their glory. ⁹ And he said to him, "All these I will give you, if you will fall down and worship me." ¹⁰ Then Jesus said to him, "Be gone, Satan! For it is written,

> *You shall worship the Lord your God*
> > *and him only shall you serve.""*

¹¹ Then the devil left him, and behold, angels came and were ministering to him.

ॐ

16.

Honor, Virtue and Self-Control

Genesis 39; Matthew 4:1-11 ESV

You have to grow up fast when you've been "shanghaied" by your siblings and sold into slavery. And that's what Joseph did. His dreams of rising to rule over his family seem kind of silly now—now that he's a slave. It seems kind of silly—except for one thing: God is with him.

Nobody in Egypt knows anything about Joseph's God—or the dreams this God has given him. But even the Egyptians who get to know Joseph know that this young man has a special knack for making things work out right—both for himself and for whoever he happens to be working for, which in this case, turns out to be an Egyptian aristocrat named Potiphar.

And then there's Potiphar's wife, whose name we do not know, but whose aim we do. She wants to commit adultery with Joseph. She might not put it that way herself—even to herself. To her, it may be something far more direct and primal.

Like Eve in the Garden of Eden,[153] this woman is mistress of all she surveys, but what she wants is the one thing she cannot have—the one thing she cannot have *without sin*, without giving up

---

[153] Genesis 2—3.

her honor and her virtue to have it—which she does give up, and still does not get what she wants—because her target turns out to be more committed to *his* honor and virtue than she is to *hers*. No wonder she goes after his "hide" when she cannot get his body.

Those who first heard and read this story would have understood immediately the tremendously important issues at stake. Our current culture, on the other hand, is clueless.

"What's the problem?" they say.

"The heart wants what the hearts wants."

"Saying 'no' is so unnatural."

"They're both adults, after all."

"It probably wasn't much of a marriage to start with."

Today, we have been conditioned to believe that self-control is both unhealthy to attempt and impossible to achieve—that virtue is a worthless relic of a bygone era—that honor is a hypocritical pretense of the "holier-than-thou" set.

None of this is true.

Virtue is behaving in ways that are pleasing to God and ultimately beneficial to you and others. Honor is the commitment to fulfill pledges and keep promises and be the person you are responsible for being to the best of your ability, whatever the cost. Self-control is the discipline we have imposed upon our personal desires so that we may be more than mere animals—more than the chaotic accumulation of our lowest impulses.

Joseph is tempted to commit adultery—to abandon his self-control—to act without virtue—to destroy his honor—and to place himself at tremendous risk of the wrath of both of his masters: the one on earth and the One in heaven. These are risks the wise young man is not willing to take.

In her seduction, the woman suggested the satisfying of physical appetites, certainly. But such unauthorized intimacy with his master's wife might also be expected to bring Joseph a greater level of power and protection than he currently enjoyed—if she chose to be loyal to him after she got what she wanted from him.

We'll never know what she would have done, because Joseph did not yield to the temptation. She did make him "pay" for making the right choice, of course. In his world as in ours, it seems, "no good deed goes unpunished."

Potiphar's wife ensured that Joseph lost everything her husband had given him. But she could not take God's presence away from Joseph, or block the blessings God would bestow upon him, or prevent the dreams he had dreamed, by God's grace, from coming true.

৵৽

And in these ways, her temptation of Joseph was not unlike Satan's temptation of Jesus centuries later.[154] Jesus was tempted, first, to satisfy his hunger—to meet nutritional needs, in His case, rather than sensual wants.

Then followed temptations to ensure His protection and extend His power—all based on the shaky assurance of the devil that he would take care of Jesus if Jesus would yield to him.

But Jesus did not yield. He resisted the temptations, exercising scripture-supported self-control to act with virtue and preserve His honor, both of which would be necessary if Jesus, like Joseph before Him, were to remain qualified to fulfill the dream God had "dreamed" for Him.[155]

Satan did not take the rejection by Jesus graciously, any more than the Egyptians seductress had taken Joseph's. Both tempter and temptress did all they could do to destroy these they could not corrupt.

But even in what looked like the direst of circumstances—prison for Joseph and the grave for Jesus—God was with them and showed them steadfast love and loyalty and gave them favor in all they did—and fulfilled the dream He had given them.

---

154 Matthew 4:1-11.
155 Hebrews 4:15; 2 Corinthians 5:21.

In Potiphar's house, everything changed when Joseph resisted temptation—and nothing changed. When he would not be seduced, Joseph lost everything his Egyptian master had given him—everything he had in the world.

But he lost nothing God had given him—nothing of eternal significance.

God was with Joseph when his brothers sold him into slavery. God was with Joseph when he was sold to Potiphar and went to work on his estate and rose to the position of overseer. God was with Joseph when he was tempted—and when he refused to give in to that temptation—and when he was falsely accused and unfairly imprisoned. And God will be with Joseph on his meteoric rise from prisoner to prime minister of all Egypt.

❧

God was with Jesus when all men praised Him[156] and when the devil tempted Him. God was with Him when He performed miracles and when the crowds grew dissatisfied and went away.[157] God was with Jesus the day they took His life,[158] and three days later, when God gave that life back to Him again and raised Jesus from rotting corpse to resurrected and reigning Christ.[159]

And God is with you to show you His steadfast love for you and to favor you and to give you His dream for your life and to strengthen your self-control when you face temptations in the world, so that you can live a life of virtue and honor in the midst of the ups and downs imposed upon you by this world that wants only to satisfy its own desires at your expense.

❧

---

[156] Luke 4:22.
[157] John 6:66.
[158] When Jesus on the Cross quotes Psalm 22:1, it is likely that He has the whole psalm in mind.
[159] Acts 2:24, 32; 10:40; 13:30; Romans 8:34.

What can Joseph—and Jesus—teach you?

When everything is going well with you in the world, you will be tempted to destroy it all. Practice self-control in order to protect your virtue and preserve your honor.

When the world does everything it can to drive you to the depths of despair,[160] it may have taken you to the very place God wants you to be so that He can fulfill the plan He has for you, and raise you up to the place He brought you into this world to occupy.[161]

Do not assume that your worldly circumstances—past, present or future—have anything to do with whether God is with you. You know He is with you, now and forever, regardless of the circumstances, because He told you so: *"Lo, I am with you always, to the end of time—and beyond."*[162]

છ્ર્જ્જ

---

[160] John 16:33.
[161] Psalm 139.
[162] Matthew 28:20, KJV.

Genesis 41:14-16, 38-40 ESV

Joseph, the son of Jacob sold by his brothers into slavery in Egypt, eventually rises from slavery and imprisonment, by the grace of God, to the highest position in the Egyptian government behind Pharaoh himself. From this position of power, Joseph will preserve his family from famine.

෧ー෧

¹⁴ Then Pharaoh sent and called Joseph, and they quickly brought him out of the pit. And when he had shaved himself and changed his clothes, he came in before Pharaoh. ¹⁵ And Pharaoh said to Joseph, "I have had a dream, and there is no one who can interpret it. I have heard it said of you that when you hear a dream you can interpret it." ¹⁶ Joseph answered Pharaoh, "It is not in me; God will give Pharaoh a favorable answer."

³⁸ And Pharaoh said to his servants, "Can we find a man like this, in whom is the Spirit of God?" ³⁹ Then Pharaoh said to Joseph, "Since God has shown you all this, there is none so discerning and wise as you are. ⁴⁰ You shall be over my house, and all my people shall order themselves as you command. Only as regards the throne will I be greater than you."

෧ー෧

Acts 2:22-24; 32-33; 36-39 ESV

On the Day of Pentecost, when the Holy Spirit came with power on the disciples of Jesus, Peter proclaimed the good news about Jesus and His Resurrection to the people of Jerusalem. And he told those who believed what he said about Jesus what to do about what they heard.

❧❧

[Peter said:]
[22] *"Men of Israel, hear these words: Jesus of Nazareth, a man attested to you by God with mighty works and wonders and signs that God did through him in your midst, as you yourselves know—* [23] *this Jesus, delivered up according to the definite plan and foreknowledge of God, you crucified and killed by the hands of lawless men.* [24] *God raised him up, loosing the pangs of death, because it was not possible for him to be held by it.*

[32] *"This Jesus God raised up, and of that we all are witnesses.* [33] *Being therefore exalted at the right hand of God, and having received from the Father the promise of the Holy Spirit, he has poured out this that you yourselves are seeing and hearing.*

[36] *"Let all the house of Israel therefore know for certain that God has made him both Lord and Christ, this Jesus whom you crucified."* [37] *Now when they heard this they were cut to the heart, and said to Peter and the rest of the apostles, "Brothers, what shall we do?"* [38] *And Peter said to them, "Repent and be baptized every one of you in the name of Jesus Christ for the forgiveness of your sins, and you will receive the gift of the Holy Spirit.* [39] *For the promise is for you and for your children and for all who are far off, everyone whom the Lord our God calls to himself."*

❧❧

17.

Dead Man Ruling

Genesis 41:14-16, 38-40
Acts 2:22-24; 32-33; 36-39 ESV

Compared to most, it was a pretty good day. Joseph began the day rotting away in an Egyptian dungeon—as good as dead for all anybody cared. He ends the day running the country—with all the perks that go with the position. Yes, all things considered: a pretty good day.

The move from prison to palace will keep Joseph busy for a while, so let's use the time to consider how a teenager, dragged into a foreign country as a slave, and then thrown in jail after he gets there) for a crime he did not commit, by the way), could suddenly find himself, 13 years later, sporting a new chariot, a new wife, a new name, and a new life as the most important man in the world.

Joseph had a lot going for him from the beginning, according to the Bible. He was trustworthy, loyal, and obedient, which earned him points with his first owner. He was also, apparently, both handsome and wholesome, a combination that didn't work out so well in dealing with his master's wife. But none of that has taken him to the pinnacle of political power and prestige.

❧

Simply put, the secret of his success is that the Spirit of God is with him. The Bible says so, and that's how Joseph explains himself to Pharaoh when he finally comes to Pharaoh's attention: *"It is not in me,"* Joseph said. "God will give you the answer you're looking for."

When Joseph was favored by his father over all the other and older sons, you could believe that God was probably with Joseph. When he had his own dreams about ruling over his brothers and his parents, he sounded like someone who might be on the spiritual fast track.

But when Joseph is attacked by his own brothers, it's a little harder to see God's presence. When they commute his death sentence to a lifetime in slavery, you would expect to see a little more divine intervention for the one God is especially attached to.

When Joseph gets to Egypt, he gets along well with Potiphar, and Potiphar's estate gets along well under Joseph, for which God is rightly given the credit.

But where is God when Mrs. Potiphar gets her mind on mischief and messes everything up for the morally upright Joseph?

And then, in prison, where Joseph is doing everything right, and for years he can't beg or buy a break, where is God?

In the Book of Acts, angels and earthquakes are opening prison doors all the time for Peter and Paul and their friends.[163] But for Joseph here in Genesis: nothing.

Only Joseph doesn't see it that way. His life is hell, but Joseph perseveres. In every situation—in every trial—Joseph has a peace that passes understanding.[164] All you can see from the outside is injustice, hardship and disappointment. And all of that is there. But there is more.

Joseph *knows* that God is with him. God was with him the day his brothers turned on him, and the day he went on sale in the

---

[163] Acts 5:17-20; 16:25-26.
[164] Philippians 4:7.

Egyptian slave market.[165] God was with him as he managed his master's affairs[166] and avoided the one his mistress wanted to have with him.[167] God was with Joseph every day in the dungeon, whether he was made the servant of other prisoners or their supervisor.[168]

৵৽৵

But how could God be with Joseph if all these bad things were happening to him? Isn't God supposed to keep bad things from happening to you?

Whatever you think the answer to that question ought to be, the truth is that God doesn't.[169] At least, not always. And for more than a few people—not very often at all, apparently.

For Joseph, the answer seems to be that God's presence and Joseph's own adversity are not incompatible. For years, Joseph will experience both at the same time. In fact, it is his certainty that God is with him that enables Joseph to endure all of his adversity—to live a life that is anything but what he wanted or expected to be living—and to live it with so much faith and hope and confidence and peace that when God does raise him up from the depths of defeat to the highest place of honor and opportunity, Joseph is able to step into his new assignment as though he has been preparing for it all his life—which he has.

Joseph does not look to what has happened—or is happening—to him in life to determine whether God is present in his life or not. On the contrary, Joseph allows a certainty of God's uninterrupted presence with him to define the meaning of every experience in his life, and to supply him with the most appropriate response to every challenge he faces.

---

[165] Genesis 39:2.
[166] Genesis 39:5.
[167] Genesis 39:9.
[168] Genesis 39:21, 23.
[169] Acts 9:15-16.

Where his father Jacob, when *he* was about Joseph's age, would wake up one morning at Bethel, shocked to realize that *"God was in this place and I did not know it,"*[170] Joseph has awakened every morning in a foreign and hostile Egypt—enslaved and alone—knowing already and all the time that his God—Who is also the God of his father Jacob—as He was of Isaac and Abraham—is with him. In Egypt or in Canaan—at home or in prison—Joseph's God is with him.

But why did his God—this God in Whom Joseph had placed all his trust, despite all he had lost—why did this God Who apparently loves Joseph so much let him lose so much—endure so much—suffer so much?

☜☞

Joseph himself did not know. But beginning today, he will begin to find out. Today, his 13-year nightmare is coming to an end, and his childhood dreams—never forgotten in all that time because God had given them—begin to be fulfilled. Or rather, Joseph begins to see their fulfillment, because God has been arranging their fulfillment all the time.

God was fulfilling them *through* Joseph's betrayal and *through* his forced march to Egypt. God was fulfilling the dreams by allowing Joseph to learn the agricultural business of Potiphar's estate. God was fulfilling Joseph's dreams by preserving Joseph's reputation for integrity and then positioning him in the very prison where God would eventually give him the opportunity and the ability to interpret the dreams of Pharaoh's officials. God was fulfilling the dream when He broke through all Pharaoh's gatekeepers to give the Egyptian king a message in *his* dreams that only Joseph could explain.

And now God has elevated Joseph from prisoner to prime minister—a fair day's work. So now everybody in Pharaoh's

---

[170] Genesis 28:10-17, NIV.

entourage can see what Joseph knew all along: His God is with him. In the days to come, all Egypt will see it, as Joseph puts God's plan for their salvation into practice.

And in seven years, with the onset of the coming famine, the whole world will start finding out who Joseph is and what his God has done to save the world—a world that includes a clan of shepherds whose leader still grieves the loss of his favorite son over 20 years before, a son who dreamed dreams.

৵৽৽

Has your life turned out like you thought it would when you were young?

Probably not. Life seldom does. Dreams are so often deferred and then discarded. We make too many trips to "Egypt"—the land of lost hopes and wasted years.

Yet even there, your God has been with you. The proof is not in how many heartaches you have been spared in your life, but in how many you have been enabled to surmount. Do not measure how far you have fallen from where you wanted to be as a sign of God's absence. It is the distance He has raised us from where we have fallen that traces the footprints of His presence.

God was present with Joseph in the midst of his suffering because it was his suffering that served the cause of the world's—and his family's—salvation. Though God does not will the evil that we do or that is done to us, the God Who is present with us will use everything about us—even the injuries, the regrets, and the failures—to work out His will for us and for others, if we will let Him.

৵৽৽

We have seen this truth played out in Joseph and in One Who is like Joseph, but infinitely greater. Where Joseph was *like* a man raised from the dead to rule, Peter at Pentecost proclaims Another Who actually *was* raised from the dead to rule:

151

"...you...put him to death by nailing him to the cross. But God raised him from the dead.... He has received from the Father the promised Holy Spirit and has poured out what you now see and hear.... God has made this Jesus...both Lord and Christ."

One day He's dead, and then, all of a sudden, He is Lord of all. And if you know that—if you believe that—your whole life—every bit of it—will be different.

God was with Joseph—God was in Christ[171]—and He is with you and in you now—now and forever.[172]

❧

---

[171] 2 Corinthians 5:19.
[172] Matthew 28:20.

Genesis 45:1-8; 50:15-20 ESV

45 *¹ Then Joseph could not control himself before all those who stood by him. He cried, "Make everyone go out from me." So no one stayed with him when Joseph made himself known to his brothers. ² And he wept aloud, so that the Egyptians heard it, and the household of Pharaoh heard it. ³ And Joseph said to his brothers, "I am Joseph! Is my father still alive?" But his brothers could not answer him, for they were dismayed at his presence.*

⁴ So Joseph said to his brothers, "Come near to me, please." And they came near. And he said, "I am your brother, Joseph, whom you sold into Egypt. ⁵ And now do not be distressed or angry with yourselves because you sold me here, for God sent me before you to preserve life. ⁶ For the famine has been in the land these two years, and there are yet five years in which there will be neither plowing nor harvest. ⁷ And God sent me before you to preserve for you a remnant on earth, and to keep alive for you many survivors. ⁸ So it was not you who sent me here, but God. He has made me a father to Pharaoh, and lord of all his house and ruler over all the land of Egypt."

50 *¹⁵ When Joseph's brothers saw that their father was dead, they said, "It may be that Joseph will hate us and pay us back for all the evil that we did to him." ¹⁶ So they sent a message to Joseph, saying, "Your father gave this command before he died: ¹⁷ 'Say to Joseph, "Please forgive the transgression of your brothers and their sin, because they did evil to you."' And now, please forgive the transgression of the servants of the God of your father." Joseph wept when they spoke to him. ¹⁸ His brothers also came and fell down before him and said, "Behold, we are your servants." ¹⁹ But Joseph said to them, "Do not fear, for am I in the place of God? ²⁰ As for you, you meant evil against me, but God meant it for good, to bring it about that many people should be kept alive, as they are today."*

છ~જી

Luke 23:1-4, 20-25, 34-43 ESV

¹ Then the whole company of them arose and brought [Jesus] before Pilate.
² And they began to accuse him, saying, "We found this man misleading our
nation and forbidding us to give tribute to Caesar, and saying that he himself
is Christ, a king." ³ And Pilate asked him, "Are you the King of the Jews?"
And he answered him, "You have said so." ⁴ Then Pilate said to the chief
priests and the crowds, "I find no guilt in this man."

²⁰ Pilate addressed them once more, desiring to release Jesus, ²¹ but they
kept shouting, "Crucify, crucify him!" ²² A third time he said to them, "Why?
What evil has he done? I have found in him no guilt deserving death. I will
therefore punish and release him." ²³ But they were urgent, demanding with
loud cries that he should be crucified. And their voices prevailed. ²⁴ So Pilate
decided that their demand should be granted. ²⁵ He released the man who had
been thrown into prison for insurrection and murder, for whom they asked, but
he delivered Jesus over to their will.

³⁴ And Jesus said, "Father, forgive them, for they know not what they do."
And they cast lots to divide his garments. ³⁵ And the people stood by, watching,
but the rulers scoffed at him, saying, "He saved others; let him save himself, if
he is the Christ of God, his Chosen One!" ³⁶ The soldiers also mocked him,
coming up and offering him sour wine ³⁷ and saying, "If you are the King of the
Jews, save yourself!" ³⁸ There was also an inscription over him, "This is the
King of the Jews."

³⁹ One of the criminals who were hanged railed at him, saying, "Are you
not the Christ? Save yourself and us!" ⁴⁰ But the other rebuked him, saying,
"Do you not fear God, since you are under the same sentence of condemnation?
⁴¹ And we indeed justly, for we are receiving the due reward of our deeds; but
this man has done nothing wrong."

⁴² And he said, "Jesus, remember me when you come into your kingdom."
⁴³ And he said to him, "Truly, I say to you, today you will be with me in
paradise."

18.

Our Evil—God's Good

Genesis 45:1-8; 50:15-20
Luke 23:1-4, 20-26, 35-43 ESV

A dozen men in an ornate room. All others have been sent away. Ten of these men—full-grown, full-bearded men—clearly share a common heritage. They all wear the same simple garb of the shepherd. They all speak a language foreign to what is normally heard in this room.

The 10 men also share a secret—the secret of an old evil they committed whose memory will not go away. On this day, in this room, they share the worried look of men who sense danger but cannot see it.

Before them sits a young, clean-shaven man, whose dress and manner set him apart. He is arrayed in a robe and ring of royalty. His manner conveys that calm assurance of one who knows himself to be the master of all he surveys. This is *his* room. He looks at these foreigners and sees their fear. It does not surprise him; he created it—on purpose.

There is a twelfth man in the room, but he is hardly more than a boy. He wears the clothing of the 10 who brought him, but if he were cleaned up a bit, he would bear an uncanny resemblance to the regal young man—the man they all fear.

What they do not know is that the stranger before them is *not* a stranger. He knows them—and he knows their secret. And he knows something else: He knows that the secret evil they did had in it the seeds of God's salvation.

⇛⇚

A dozen men alone together in an ornate room, and the stranger who is not a stranger has decided that it is time to speak.

"I am Joseph."

And with those words, the regal figure explodes the secret and turns the world and the future of all 12 of them upside down.

"I am the brother you left for dead—and now I rule all of Egypt."

The 10 older men are terrified. They realize immediately they are in far greater jeopardy than they had imagined. They deserve the greatest punishment possible for what they did to Joseph their brother, and they know they are powerless to prevent the seemingly risen-from-the-dead Joseph from exacting his just revenge.

But in the years since their sin, they have come to acknowledge—at least among themselves—that what they did was sin. And more, they have come to grieve their evil and the pain it has caused their father and their family. And now to their amazement, because they have confessed their sin and demonstrated their remorse—the one they sinned against is willing—and able—to forgive them.

The brothers know that what they did to Joseph was evil. They know it, and Joseph knows it, and God knows it. But the miraculous thing is that in the all-knowing, all-powerful, redemptive hands of God, their evil has been turned into God's good. God has used their own sin to save them.

⇛⇚

Now, fast forward some 16 centuries, and see their descendants conspiring to give another brother over to foreigners—to arrange His death. The chief priests and elders (the "older brothers" of their day) don't like what this impertinent Upstart has to tell them. And they don't appreciate His claiming a special relationship with their Father—their Heavenly Father.

So, like Joseph's brothers, they decide to do their brother Jesus in. In the process, He is stripped of His clothes, mocked and derided for His helplessness, and left for dead in a hole in the ground. It is evil, but they do what they do, and are prepared to live with their sin, because they think they have gotten away with murder.

But it doesn't work out that way, because there is a God Who is watching—and working out His will in and through the affairs of men—even through their evil deeds. Nothing that man has done remains "done" in the face of a God Who "un-does" and "re-does" all things according to His holy and eternal will. The evil we do does not remain forever—though the guilt of it may.

The evil does not remain as evil because God is not willing to allow evil to endure in the world that He is ever re-creating.

But what of those who do the evil? What of the brothers of Joseph—the countrymen of Jesus—and us?

Even if God redeems the evil deeds we have done, the deeds were evil when we did them, for we intended them so. And they would have remained so, except for God's grace redeeming them. We could never undo the evil we have done—and seldom would we have wanted to, even if we could, as long as we were not suffering the painful consequences our actions deserved.

But in order to redeem our evil, God first had to absorb it—to experience it ultimately as sin against Him. That's why the Psalmist would say to God, *"Against You, and You only, have I sinned."*[173] That's where every sin ends up: in the heart of God.

---

[173] Psalm 51:4 ESV.

And what is God's response to our sin against Him?

Well, contrary to the popular thinking, He does not condone it. He cannot—and remain a just God.

This good God cannot condone our sins, but He can forgive us. He can and does include us in His glorious and gracious work of redemption. God redeems sin *and* sinner—if they will submit to Him.

The sin is easy. It always submits to the power and wisdom and will of God's redemptive work. Once done, a sinful act is inanimate—a lifeless thing, subject to God's acting upon it.

But the sinner is something else—some-*one* else—a being with a will of his own—able and inclined to oppose God both by doing evil, and then by resisting God's efforts to redeem him from what he has done—and from his desire to do it again.

But there comes a day for everyone when resistance to God will end. That day may be delayed so long by the willful waywardness of the sinner that the possibility of redemption is gone.

The brothers of Joseph were afraid they had reached that point when they discovered that Joseph was not dead, but alive. They feared they had reached that point again with the death of their father, Jacob. They were afraid that the victim of their sin was about to become the instrument of their punishment.

But it turns out that Joseph had come to love them so much—despite their sin against him—that he gave them time to repent. And when he saw that they had repented, he was able to exercise the forgiveness he was waiting and wanting to bestow.

❧

And in the same way on the Cross, Jesus would look at those who brought about His Crucifixion and pray to God for their forgiveness—based on their ignorance. Consider what an odd prayer it is: *"Father, forgive them, for they know not what they do."*

It would seem they knew exactly what they were doing. Pilate—a foreigner who didn't care a fig about their religion—tried repeatedly to talk them out of it, but they were determined to destroy this Brother they despised.

But Jesus was right about their not knowing, because they didn't understand that what they meant for evil, God meant for good. In the hands of God, their evil became good, just as the brothers' act of betrayal against Joseph became, in the hands of God, the source of *their* salvation.

What is Jesus praying on the Cross?

He is asking God to delay judgment until those who brought about His death can see the good that God will bring out of it, and understand God's purpose in it, and repent, so that God's forgiveness can play out in their lives.

Jesus prays that the good that God brings out of His death—an evil they brought about—will be so clearly and powerfully revealed, that God's redemption of their sin—and of other sinners—through the Cross—will also eventually bring about the change of heart in them that enables God's redemption and salvation to work within them, too.

❧

Joseph, who was the victim of his brothers' sin, has seen God redeem the evil done to him, and so he understands what they do not: They are forgiven—and, through their contrition, they enable themselves to receive that forgiveness. The debt of their sin has been cancelled and a new life lies before them.

And now, we stand like them, sinners of sins, facing the One against Whom we have sinned, certain of our guilt. If we are willing to confess it—we may know ourselves redeemed and restored by the One Who died because of—and for—our sins. We humble ourselves before the One Who was humbled by the sins of mankind, and Who before that, was humbled by His desire to serve

His—*our*—Father,[174] the God Who sent Jesus ahead—as long before, He had sent Joseph—to endure the evil inflicted upon Him in order to prepare our way of salvation—to preserve us alive when we should have suffered what He suffered for us, instead.

Joseph was not God, but God was with him and turned the evil of his brothers into good.

Jesus was God, and God was with Him in a way that was like—but infinitely greater than—the way God was with Joseph.

And the God Who was with and in—and *was*—Jesus has taken the sins, not just of 10 brothers, but of the whole world, and stands ready and able to give everyone in the world the means to live, not just through a few years of famine, but forever.[175]

And for that reason, let us remember our sins, and turn them and ourselves over to God, so that like the sinner on the cross beside Jesus, we may ask to be—and know that we certainly are and will be—remembered by Him in the kingdom to which He came after His Crucifixion—that we are and will be forgiven of all our sins—our evil—that has, in Jesus, been transformed into God's good.

෴

---

174 Philippians 2:7.
175 Hebrews 9:24-28.

From the Book of Exodus

Exodus 8:1-15 ESV

¹ Then the LORD *said to Moses, "Go in to Pharaoh and say to him, 'Thus says the* LORD, *"Let my people go, that they may serve me. ² But if you refuse to let them go, behold, I will plague all your country with frogs. ³ The Nile shall swarm with frogs that shall come up into your house and into your bedroom and on your bed and into the houses of your servants and your people, and into your ovens and your kneading bowls. ⁴ The frogs shall come up on you and on your people and on all your servants."'" ⁵ And the* LORD *said to Moses, "Say to Aaron, 'Stretch out your hand with your staff over the rivers, over the canals and over the pools, and make frogs come up on the land of Egypt!'" ⁶ So Aaron stretched out his hand over the waters of Egypt, and the frogs came up and covered the land of Egypt. ⁷ But the magicians did the same by their secret arts and made frogs come up on the land of Egypt.*

⁸ Then Pharaoh called Moses and Aaron and said, "Plead with the LORD *to take away the frogs from me and from my people, and I will let the people go to sacrifice to the* LORD.*" ⁹ Moses said to Pharaoh, "Be pleased to command me when I am to plead for you and for your servants and for your people, that the frogs be cut off from you and your houses and be left only in the Nile." ¹⁰ And he said, "Tomorrow." Moses said, "Be it as you say, so that you may know that there is no one like the* LORD *our God. ¹¹ The frogs shall go away from you and your houses and your servants and your people. They shall be left only in the Nile." ¹² So Moses and Aaron went out from Pharaoh, and Moses cried to the* LORD *about the frogs, as he had agreed with Pharaoh. ¹³ And the* LORD *did according to the word of Moses. The frogs died out in the houses, the courtyards, and the fields. ¹⁴ And they gathered them together in heaps, and the land stank. ¹⁵ But when Pharaoh saw that there was a respite, he hardened his heart and would not listen to them, as the* LORD *had said.*

⊰•⊱

Luke 13:10-17 ESV

[10] Now [Jesus] was teaching in one of the synagogues on the Sabbath. [11] And behold, there was a woman who had had a disabling spirit for eighteen years. She was bent over and could not fully straighten herself. [12] When Jesus saw her, he called her over and said to her, "Woman, you are freed from your disability." [13] And he laid his hands on her, and immediately she was made straight, and she glorified God. [14] But the ruler of the synagogue, indignant because Jesus had healed on the Sabbath, said to the people, "There are six days in which work ought to be done. Come on those days and be healed, and not on the Sabbath day." [15] Then the Lord answered him, "You hypocrites! Does not each of you on the Sabbath untie his ox or his donkey from the manger and lead it away to water it? [16] And ought not this woman, a daughter of Abraham whom Satan bound for eighteen years, be loosed from this bond on the Sabbath day?" [17] As he said these things, all his adversaries were put to shame, and all the people rejoiced at all the glorious things that were done by him.

త్రోత్తు

19.

One More Night with the Frogs

Exodus 8:1-15; Luke 13:10-17 ESV

Forty years ago, I was a young, single seminary student, just out of college, beginning my preparation for ministry. I had not yet written or even preached a sermon. Many of my classmates were older men who took courses during the week and went home to their families and churches on the weekends. I may have learned more about ministry from them "after hours" than I did from my professors in class.

One evening over dinner, the talk turned to the subject of sermon titles, and one of these men said he had a sermon he called, "One More Night with the Frogs." I never got a chance to hear or read that sermon, but I never forgot the title. I've always wanted to preach a sermon with such a title, and 40 years later, as our "Preach-through-the-Bible" plan brings us to the Plagues of Egypt, that's what I propose to do.

The title refers to Pharaoh's unusual answer to Moses' question after the second plague—the overrunning of Egypt by frogs. Moses asked when Pharaoh would like him to start praying to God to "turn off" this plague. You would think that if you're "plagued" by something—if your whole country is plagued by it—you would want immediate relief—"Right now!" relief.

"When?" says Moses.

And Pharaoh answers, "Tomorrow"—which is another way of saying: "I'm willing to live with the problem one more night."

You know the background: God's people are enslaved in Egypt. They've been there for hundreds of years. Egypt is, at the time, the most powerful country on earth. Pharaoh, the king who rules over Egypt, is the most powerful *man* in the world. At least, everybody assumes he is—including Pharaoh himself.

If Pharaoh wants the children of Israel to be his slaves, who's to stop him?

Everybody in Egypt—including, probably, the majority of God's people—thinks the answer is: "Nobody."

But God has a different answer: "I will stop him; I have heard My people's cry and I will set them free."[176]

The real question is: How much power will God have to take away from Pharaoh before this extremely powerful man will realize that this God he does not know is a great deal more powerful than he is—before Pharaoh, voluntarily or otherwise, gives up his hold on God's people? How much will God have to do to Pharaoh and his country before Pharaoh will do what God is telling him to do?

There will be ten plagues in all,[177] and they will get progressively distasteful and destructive until, finally, Pharaoh will have no choice but to beg God's people to leave what's left of Egypt—and slaves will walk freely out of a once awesome empire, now in ruins.[178]

But early in the process, Pharaoh is still more concerned about holding on to as much of his power as possible than about ending the suffering of his kingdom as soon as possible.

Pharaoh can't prevent the plagues from happening—for all his supposed power. He can't end the plagues once they've started—no human power could.

---

[176] Exodus 3:7-10.
[177] Exodus 5—12.
[178] Exodus 12:31-32.

Of course, he could have prevented the plagues—or ended them at any time—if he had been willing to acknowledge and submit to the Power greater than his own—the power of this incredible God of the people Pharaoh held in bondage against their God's will.

❧

So, are you dealing with any "plagues" right now? Got anything "froggy" overrunning everything everywhere you turn and stinking up your life? What is it that God is making you miserable about while He waits for you to turn over control of your life to Him? What do you keep saying "Tomorrow" about, when, if you would let Him, God would make it all right, right now?

Addicts of various kinds are always saying, "I'll stop tomorrow. I'll get help tomorrow."

But that tomorrow never comes.

Of course, it doesn't have to be some devastating addiction. Anything you hold on to for yourself that you ought to turn over to God can take you to the place where God will demand it and "plague" you until you let Him have His way with it—and with you.

We all want to rule over as much of our lives—as much of our worlds—as possible. The trouble is, it's not your world—it's not your life. Your life and your world belong to the One Who created them. They are God's, and He wants them. God wants to rule over your world in order to bring order out of its chaos. And He wants to rule over your life, to set you free from the bondage that any other ruler will force you into—including you.

Why would Pharaoh endure even one more night of unnecessary suffering? Why would he subject his family, his friends—his whole community—to even a minute more of their shared nightmare?

❧

The simple answer is "pride."

Pharaoh doesn't want to look weak, even though God has revealed just how weak he is, underneath all the outward trappings of power: "If I don't have the power to deal with the plague before me, maybe I can still pretend that I do, and those I have deceived and ruled over may still be impressed with me.

"Or maybe I can bargain with God. Maybe I don't have to give up all of my power to this God. Maybe He really doesn't require all that He demands.

"Or maybe I can fool this God. I'll tell Him what He wants to hear and, if He takes the plague away, I'm home free."

Promises are certainly easier and cheaper to make than they are to keep—especially the ones you make to God.

God kept His promise. The frogs died the day Pharaoh selected: tomorrow. God keeps His promises, no matter what. But when Pharaoh reneged on his promise to God, the plagues resumed, and every new one was harsher than the one before it.

Pharaoh acted in pride. And God humbled him completely, and systematically destroyed every semblance of his power. Pharaoh tried to bargain with God like some chronic and compulsive gambler, and his losses quickly multiplied well beyond his ability to make good.

The one who thought he could fool God was himself shown to be a fool.

⬦⬦

Why do we tell God, "Tomorrow"?

Does it matter why?

The answer to God's "When?" should always be "Now!" "Right now!"

"When will you let Me rule over you?"

"Now, Lord. Right now!"

"When will you obey Me?"

"Now, Lord. Right now!"

"When do you want Me to stop the pressure I'm applying to get you to do what I want you to do?"

"Now, Lord. Do that now because I will do what You command me to do from right now on."

"When you submit to Me, I will set you free. When will you let Me set you free?"

"Now, Lord. Right now."

You see, all this plague business was about getting the one holding God's people captive to let them go free from their bondage, so God could have them back.

But here's the funny thing: when Pharaoh told God, "Tomorrow," God was prepared "to set Pharaoh free" as well.

God set Pharaoh free from the frogs, and would have set him free a day earlier, if he had asked, or saved him from suffering the frogs and all the other plagues at all, if Pharaoh had done what God told him to do—if he had submitted to the God Who can set Egyptians free from their bondage to their illusions of power as easily as He can set His Chosen People free from the actual oppression of the Egyptians.

But Pharaoh hardened his heart.

ॐ∘ॐ

It's so simple, really, when everybody wants to make it out to be complicated. Harden your heart against what God wants from you—and *for* you—and you can look forward to being plagued. God is working His will in each of us and *will* have His way.

The problem with hardening your heart against God's will, of course, is that a hard heart is more likely to be broken. It will *have* to be. It is the surrendered, submissive heart that God can fill with His powerful Presence and protect from the plagues the world would inflict upon it.

A "tomorrow" heart is actually a hardened or hardening heart. The "now" heart is the spiritually healthy heart that will know the liberation of God's love.

That's why, when the people in Jesus' day were saying, "Wait till tomorrow,"[179] Jesus was saying, "No! Now is the time."[180] When thousands were hungry, He told His disciples, "We'll feed them now."[181] When they tried to turn little children away, He said, "I'll see them now."[182]

When the religious leaders wanted a woman in bondage to a bad back to come back tomorrow, Jesus would not let her spend one more night with her infirmity.[183] "Woman, you are free!" Jesus said to her, just as His heavenly Father said to her ancestors in Egypt, despite what the Pharaoh tried to say.

The rulers in the synagogue were just as eager to hold on to their power as Pharaoh had been to hold onto his. But they could not heal the poor woman any more than Pharaoh could keep the plagues away. And they could not stop Jesus from healing her any more than Pharaoh could stop the Exodus. They were all dealing with a Power far greater than their own.

God sent Moses and Aaron, His servants, and Jesus, His Son, to set His people free. And no matter how God's opponents tried to delay or avoid God's will, those who were bound, either in slavery or in sin, were set free.

And the only ones who weren't—who were left to face God's wrath instead—were those who were unwilling to submit to His power and receive His redemptive love.

ॐॐ

Why would anybody spend one more night than necessary with any plague?

"When do you want the nightmare to be over?" says God.

---

179 Mark 3:1-6.
180 John 5:24-25.
181 Matthew 15:32.
182 Matthew 19:12-13.
183 Luke 13:10-16.

Tomorrow?

Don't be silly.

Now is the time to stop struggling with God—to stop hurting—to give in to God and let Him set you free.

When?

Now.

&-&

Exodus 11:1, 4-8; 12:31-33, 51 ESV

Moses and Aaron went to the Egyptian king as God directed, demanding that the king release God's people from bondage. The king refused, setting up a contest between the powers of Egypt and the power of God in which God sent a series of plagues upon Egypt until the king relented. The passage below refers to the last of the 10 plagues, and the king's response to it.

ॐ•ॐ

11 *¹ The* LORD *said to Moses, "Yet one plague more I will bring upon Pharaoh and upon Egypt. Afterward he will let you go from here. When he lets you go, he will drive you away completely."*

⁴ So Moses said, "Thus says the LORD*: 'About midnight I will go out in the midst of Egypt, ⁵ and every firstborn in the land of Egypt shall die, from the firstborn of Pharaoh who sits on his throne, even to the firstborn of the slave girl who is behind the handmill, and all the firstborn of the cattle. ⁶ There shall be a great cry throughout all the land of Egypt, such as there has never been, nor ever will be again. ⁷ But not a dog shall growl against any of the people of Israel, either man or beast, that you may know that the* LORD *makes a distinction between Egypt and Israel.' ⁸ And all these your servants shall come down to me and bow down to me, saying, 'Get out, you and all the people who follow you.' And after that I will go out." And he went out from Pharaoh in hot anger.*

12 *³¹ Then [Pharaoh] summoned Moses and Aaron by night and said, "Up, go out from among my people, both you and the people of Israel; and go, serve the* LORD*, as you have said. ³² Take your flocks and your herds, as you have said, and be gone, and bless me also!" ³³ The Egyptians were urgent with the people to send them out of the land in haste. For they said, "We shall all be dead."*

⁵¹ And on that very day the Lord brought the people of Israel out of the land of Egypt by their hosts.

ॐ•ॐ

John 8:27-36 ESV

Jesus is talking with some of His fellow Jews about His identity and His relationship with God, and about the authority for what He is teaching. He emphasizes that by telling them the truth about God, He is freeing them from their bondage to sin.

ॐ

²⁷ *They did not understand that [Jesus] had been speaking to them about the Father.* ²⁸ *So Jesus said to them, "When you have lifted up the Son of Man, then you will know that I am he, and that I do nothing on my own authority, but speak just as the Father taught me.* ²⁹ *And he who sent me is with me. He has not left me alone, for I always do the things that are pleasing to him."* ³⁰ *As he was saying these things, many believed in him.*

³¹ *So Jesus said to the Jews who had believed him, "If you abide in my word, you are truly my disciples,* ³² *and you will know the truth, and the truth will set you free."* ³³ *They answered him, "We are offspring of Abraham and have never been enslaved to anyone. How is it that you say, 'You will become free'?"*

³⁴ *Jesus answered them, "Truly, truly, I say to you, everyone who practices sin is a slave to sin.* ³⁵ *The slave does not remain in the house forever; the son remains forever.* ³⁶ *So if the Son sets you free, you will be free indeed."*

ॐ

20.

Out of the Land of Egypt

Exodus 11:1, 4-8; 12:31-33, 51 ESV

The children of Israel are in bondage—slaves in the land of Egypt. Bondage is a bad thing. Slavery is certainly not what God had in mind when He created mankind in His image.[184] And Egypt is not the land God promised His people as the place where they would dwell.[185]

And yet, there they are: in Egypt; slaves in a foreign land. Four hundred years earlier they had gone down to Egypt, free men and their families, led by their father Jacob—Israel—to wait out a famine and live off this land that his God had raised up his long lost son, Joseph, to control.[186] Joseph invited them to come to Egypt, and God authorized them to go, because God had chosen to use Egypt to preserve His people. At the same time, God was blessing and preserving Egypt through and because of His people, Israel.

Five years later, the famine ended, but this family of God did not choose to leave the land of Egypt. When their father Jacob died, they took his body back to the land God had promised them,

---

184 Genesis 1:26-30.
185 Genesis 12:1.
186 Genesis 46:1-7.

and they buried Jacob alongside Abraham and Sarah, Isaac and Rebekah.[187] But the sons of Israel did not stay in the land of promise. They went back to live in the land of Egypt.

And when Joseph, the brother God sent ahead of them to deliver them from starvation and death, died himself, they did not even take him home to bury him.[188]

The children of Israel had grown comfortable in the land of Egypt, and they remained so, generation after generation, until they had lived so long in Egypt that none of them remembered—or cared—that this was not their home.[189] The one who remembered—and cared—was a king—a pharaoh who rose to power and did two things: He made the children of Israel, now a great multitude of people, want, finally, to leave the land of Egypt—and he made it impossible for them to do so.[190] The king of Egypt made the children of God the slaves of men. Then they knew that Egypt was not their home.

⇛⇝

One who has been enslaved does not forget the experience of bondage. The children of Israel would be freed by the mighty power of God from the choking grip of Pharaoh. And Moses,[191] and the prophets after him,[192] and the psalmists before and after them,[193] would never let the people forget what happened to their ancestors—and to them—in the land of Egypt. And so the Bible never stops talking about Egypt.

In the pages of God's Word, Egypt becomes more than just the country to the southwest.

---

[187] Genesis 50:7-14.
[188] Genesis 50:26.
[189] Exodus 1:7.
[190] Exodus 1:8-12.
[191] Deuteronomy 5:15.
[192] Jeremiah 7:25; Ezekiel 20:6.
[193] Psalm 81:10; 106:7, 21.

For every child of God, there is "a land of promise" and "a land of Egypt." But you won't find these places on any map. You can't "Google" them. They are not geographical; they are metaphorical.

"The land of promise" is the place God provides for His people—the place where God is—where He dwells with those He has chosen, and they dwell in peace and safety with Him. "The land of promise" is the place flowing with milk and honey, which means the blessings—material and spiritual—God bestows upon the children He loves—the sons and daughters He has made His own. "The land of promise" is home for the children of God.

"The land of Egypt" is not our home. In fact, it is an alien land that is far from being our home, though we experience it as very often very close at hand. "The land of Egypt" is not what God has promised His children. But that doesn't stop this metaphorical "Egypt" from making lots of promises. The promises of this Egypt are alluring—and empty. It presents itself as a land of luxury. It is ultimately a land of bondage, sorrow and death.

Let's clarify: "the land of Egypt" is, for the Bible, not just a place on a map; it is a code word—an image—for every way of living that is not ordained or approved by God. "The land of Egypt" is every moral system that ignores or opposes the revealed will of God—every social, civic or cultural clique, every government official or agency, every media outlet or celebrity that would challenge God for the authority to direct your life. It is every temptation that offers the easy life of earthly pleasures and, in the end, gives only disappointment, bondage, sorrow and death.

ॐ

Every morning when you wake up, you will choose whether you will spend that day in "the land of promise" with God, or in "the land of Egypt," subject—whether you realize it or not—to Pharaoh's rule. What the Bible tells us is that when you make your home in Egypt, lured by its (apparent) benefits, one day, Egypt will decide that *you* belong to *it*. And where, for a time, you may have been allowed to enjoy the creature comforts of this foreign land, there will come a time when this Egypt will make you its captured creature, and comfort itself at your expense.

You see, Egypt only cares about Egypt. Egypt always wants to own those who inhabit it. In Egypt, everyone and everything is "property." Egypt only cares about how it can use God's people for its own benefit, whether that means making one of them a prime minister or all of them a slave.

People slip into slavery in this metaphorical Egypt every day. They don't mean to. They don't want to. They never think they will. But that's what happens in "the land of Egypt" to anyone who chooses to live there, instead of going home to "the land of promise." Egypt enslaves. It is the land of bondage...

☙◈❧

...except when the God of "the land of promise" decides to send His people into Egypt to protect them, or to bring them out of bondage there to prove to Egypt and the world—and to the slaves He brings out—that He is the God Who is greater than all gods, and, as such, can do whatever pleases Him. And what pleases this great God today is to send a scruffy, stuttering, seemingly helpless old shepherd to the mighty king of Egypt to order him to set the captives free.

And though the seemingly powerful Egypt scoffs at the simple shepherd and the message he conveys, the land and its leaders will be plagued into submission by the God for Whom this shepherd—Moses—speaks.

Egypt enslaves—and the God of the slaves of Egypt liberates. You know where it ends up: sudden, shocking death! Death of every Egyptian firstborn. Death in every part of Egypt, and so widespread that no one is left to comfort anybody else. That's the worst of it—but not the half of it.

Before death there was bad, bloody water and beastly frogs everywhere—gnats and flies so dense they were like the dust of the earth—then disease and weather disasters. Hordes of locusts turned the sky as dark as night—and then the sky and everything in it went dark all on their own.

And finally, Egypt was destroyed; God's gracious gift of Creation was reversed—order was returned to chaos—and the children of Israel marched out of their slavery—out of "the land of Egypt"—like a victorious army on parade. But they had not fought the battle; it was their God Who fought it for them—Who freed them from the Pharaoh they could not fight or flee.

ॐ∽

Centuries later, this liberating God will recall what He had done in words recorded by the prophet Hosea: *"...out of Egypt I called my son."*[194] Out of the land of bondage, God called "Israel," the patriarch personified in the multitude of people who descended from him. God called His people out of Egypt because Egypt was not their home, and slavery to the power of Egypt was not the purpose for which He made them the children of His promise. And if Egypt had to taste God's plagues to bring about this liberation, it was only because they would not obey God and let His people go.

But the word in Hosea is not merely history. It is also prophecy, for the day will come when God will again "call a son out of Egypt," His only begotten Son.[195] God will send His Firstborn to Egypt to protect Him for a time, and then call Him back to "the land of promise" when it is time for Jesus to free the captives held in bondage in the metaphorical Egypt of sin.

And to destroy the hold of this "Egypt," to "break the power of cancelled sin,"[196] it is *God's* Firstborn Who will die this time—

---

[194] Hosea 11:1, NIV.

[195] Matthew 2:19-21.

[196] From "O, For a Thousand Tongues to Sing," Charles Wesley, 1739.

179

while death passes over all the sinners of the world.[197] God has sent another simple Shepherd to confront the power that holds His people in bondage, and this Good Shepherd[198] will become the sacrificial Lamb[199] Who brakes their bonds and "sets the prisoners free."[200]

The metaphorical Egypt is all around us. Its leader—the devil—has been defeated by God. He has no power to hold those God has freed. But this Egypt is a land filled with hardened hearts and it continues to lure the unwary into bondage.

And so, it will suffer the plagues appropriate to its sins. All the things this world in rebellion against God has offered as the substitute for truth—to appeal to those who belong in "the land of promise"—will reap the due consequences they deserve.[201] In some cases, they are reaping them already.

Children of God, the Egypts of this world are not your home. They are not the land God has promised you. Do not settle for lives that promise ease and comfort while measuring you for the chains of bondage.

God calls you out of Egypt. The bonds of sin have been broken. Your God has set you free. Rise up and go! Come home to the land He has promised.

∽✥

---

197 Romans 5:19.
198 John 10:11.
199 John 1:29.
200 Again, "O, For a Thousand Tongues to Sing."
201 Galatians 6:7-8.

Exodus 19:1-8, 16-19; 20:18-21 ESV

God delivered the children of Israel from bondage and then
from Pharaoh's army. God parted the sea and His people passed
safely through on dry ground. Now they have come to Mount
Sinai, the holy mountain, to meet their God.

❧

19 *¹ On the third new moon after the people of Israel had gone out of the
land of Egypt, on that day they came into the wilderness of Sinai. ² They set
out from Rephidim and came into the wilderness of Sinai, and they encamped
in the wilderness. There Israel encamped before the mountain, ³ while Moses
went up to God. The LORD called to him out of the mountain, saying, "Thus
you shall say to the house of Jacob, and tell the people of Israel: ⁴ 'You yourselves
have seen what I did to the Egyptians, and how I bore you on eagles' wings
and brought you to myself. ⁵ Now therefore, if you will indeed obey my voice
and keep my covenant, you shall be my treasured possession among all peoples,
for all the earth is mine; ⁶ and you shall be to me a kingdom of priests and a
holy nation.' These are the words that you shall speak to the people of Israel."*

*⁷ So Moses came and called the elders of the people and set before them all
these words that the LORD had commanded him. ⁸ All the people answered
together and said, "All that the LORD has spoken we will do." And Moses
reported the words of the people to the LORD.*

*¹⁶ On the morning of the third day there were thunders and lightnings and
a thick cloud on the mountain and a very loud trumpet blast, so that all the
people in the camp trembled. ¹⁷ Then Moses brought the people out of the camp
to meet God, and they took their stand at the foot of the mountain. ¹⁸ Now
Mount Sinai was wrapped in smoke because the Lord had descended on it in
fire. The smoke of it went up like the smoke of a kiln, and the whole mountain
trembled greatly. ¹⁹ And as the sound of the trumpet grew louder and louder,
Moses spoke, and God answered him in thunder.*

20 ¹⁸ *Now when all the people saw the thunder and the flashes of lightning and the sound of the trumpet and the mountain smoking, the people were afraid and trembled, and they stood far off* ¹⁹ *and said to Moses, "You speak to us, and we will listen; but do not let God speak to us, lest we die."* ²⁰ *Moses said to the people, "Do not fear, for God has come to test you, that the fear of him may be before you, that you may not sin."*

❧❧

21.

Brought Out to Meet God

Exodus 19:1-8, 16-19; 20:18-20 ESV

There are places where heaven touches earth. There are times when God comes to meet His people. There are events that re-define everything that went before and shape everything that will come after. Sinai is such a place. Sinai is such a time. And Sinai is such an event.

Three months after the children of Israel walked out of bondage in Egypt a free people, they came to the Desert of Sinai. They entered this desert and camped at the foot of the mountain that gave it its name. The children of Israel came to Mount Sinai, the holy mountain of God. Moses *led* them there, but it was God Who *brought* them, just as it was God Who delivered them from their hell on earth.

If you will recall, when God sent Moses to Egypt, the mission was more than: "Tell Pharaoh to let My people go!"[202] Their freedom from slavery and oppression was not, for God, the goal—the point. Deliverance was a means to an even greater end. When God had broken Pharaoh to the point that the king could not hold

---

[202] Exodus 5:1.

them any longer, the children of Israel were to come out of Egypt—and go to Sinai, the mountain of God.

And three days after they arrived at Mount Sinai, they would understand why they had been delivered from slavery—why they had been saved by the mighty power of God. On their third day at Sinai, the children of Israel would see heaven come down to earth. They would hear the very voice of God. They would experience an event that would leave them terrified—and transformed—because on that day, at that place, they would meet their God. Thunder and lightning—fire and smoke—heaven sounds of trumpets and the earth quakes to its core. God meets His people at Sinai.

Three days earlier, they had agreed to obey God's voice and keep His covenant. Today, Moses brings them out of camp to stand before the awesome majesty of God. And on that holy ground—in that sacred moment—God comes and chooses a people to be uniquely His among all the people of the world.

The Creator of all the earth—the *Lord* of all the earth—consecrates these "nobodies" to be His special servants—to be the go-betweens between God and the rest of mankind. God elects this nation, rather than any other nation on the earth, to be set apart for His divine purpose—not to rule over the nations, but to serve them and show them what it means to be God's people.

And when He has transformed them into what He wants them to be, God speaks to His Chosen People. Not Moses, this time, passing on God's message. God!

The people standing at the foot of Sinai hear the voice of God, and the words God speaks in their hearing begin like this: *"I am the LORD your God, who brought you out of Egypt, out of the land of slavery. You shall have no other gods before me...."*[203]

And just as God sent 10 plagues to free them; God now speaks 10 words—10 commandments—to form them. Ten Commandments, that's all that comes directly from the mouth of

---

[203] Exodus 20:1-3, NIV.

God—unfiltered and unmediated—to the children of Israel, but it is enough to send them into a panic.

"No more!" they beg. "Let Moses tell us what God says. Oh, God, please don't speak to us again. It could kill us!"

As the saying goes, "It wasn't so much *what* He said; it was the *way* He said it." And from then on, God spoke to His people through Moses—and after Moses, through priest and prophet, psalmist and sage.

৵৵৵

The ceremony goes on, there at the mountain—at Sinai. Thunder and lightning—fire and smoke—the children of Israel, terrified—Almighty God, up close and personal—and Moses in the middle.

But now, step back. Step back and look, not just at this spectacular encounter with God, but at the whole process of what God has been doing—the chain of events that began in Egypt and led to Sinai and that will soon lead away from Sinai with God in the lead and His new kingdom of priests following.

It began with deliverance from bondage—salvation from lives lost to those who lived them—salvation so powerful that it broke the death grip of the greatest power on earth—a hold no one but God could break.

God delivered people who had done nothing to deserve it. God delivered anyone who would accept the freedom He created.[204] All you had to do was let Him bring you out. But if you joined the parade out of darkness into the light, you weren't on your own when you got past the parted waters.[205] You were going somewhere. You were going to meet God.

Yes, I know: God is everywhere. But there are special places— holy, powerful, mysterious places—where God chooses to meet people in holy, powerful, mysterious ways. You see, you can let

---

[204] Exodus 12:37-38.
[205] Exodus 14:21-31.

God bring you out of bondage, but if you will not let Him bring you to the place where He is, you will have come out of one bondage just to slide into another.[206] God's purpose for saving people is not just to save people, but to bring them to meet Him.[207]

In God's process, there is deliverance, and then, there is encounter. And in that moment of divine encounter, God establishes a relationship with you. This relationship requires willing obedience *from* you and provides a new identity and mission *for* you. God comes to you and makes you His special treasure. God consecrates you as a mediator of His divine grace to every person you meet.[208] God awards you citizenship in the spiritual community He has founded to show this broken, sinful world the way to redemption.

༂

Deliverance, encounter, transformation—and only then, law. Yes, law. Commandments, statutes, ordinances, rules. The Bible is full of them. But remember, God does not impose His law; He gives it as a gift—to those He loves—and those who love Him. Deliverance—salvation—does not depend on obeying the law.[209] God delivers *before* He gives law.

Those who encounter God in the wake of their deliverance do not do so on the basis of good behavior. The encounter with God also comes *before* law. God comes to anyone who will accept His salvation and follow Him out of darkness and slavery.[210]

And transformation?

You do not become God's servant by passing a moral entrance exam. Your desire to obey the God Who delivers from bondage is sufficient to start with.

---

[206] Matthew 12:43-45.
[207] John 14:1-3, Revelation 7:9.
[208] 2 Corinthians 5:18, 20.
[209] Ephesians 2:8-9.
[210] Acts 16:31.

God gave His law to the children of Israel at Sinai so that they would know how to do what they wanted—and had already agreed—to do. God gave His Word—His Law—so that they would not be at a loss in showing the lost the way to the God they met at Sinai.

We say "Law"—meaning that nothing God says should ever be taken lightly. But you must understand that what God gave them—and gives you who have come to the mountain and met your God and accepted His holy commission—is *instruction*—*guidance*—a *framework* for being a chosen instrument who brings His grace to the world, after He has brought you out to meet Him.

By receiving and learning God's Law—His Word—and living obediently under its authority and according to its wisdom, you become a part of God's transforming labor of love for all the other people in all the other nations who have not yet allowed God to bring them out of their personal bondage to meet Him at the "Sinai"—the holy place—He has chosen for them.

Deliverance—encounter—transformation—law: the divine process.

❧

Now go back—back to the mountain where God has brought His people to meet Him.

But notice that time has moved on, to the time when God gathered His people at the foot of a new holy mountain. It, too, is a place where heaven touched earth because one day God came down on this sacred mountain to meet His people. And on this mountain, an event took place that, like the encounter with God at Mount Sinai, changed everything for everybody who came there. This new holy mountain is called Mount Calvary.[211]

---

[211] Matthew 27:33-35; Mark 15:22-24; John 19:17-18. The term used in these English passages is "Golgotha," the Aramaic name of the site of the Crucifixion. "Calvary" is the Latin translation of "Golgotha."

The place is different, but the pattern is the same: deliverance—encounter—transformation—law.

God on Calvary broke the power, not of a human tyrant, but of death itself,[212] to set the captives free. He did this, not by taking the lives of the oppressors, but by giving His own as a perfect sacrifice.[213] And from their bondage, God brought out, not just those enslaved in one corner of the globe, but the lost souls of all the earth—all who would follow Him out into true freedom.

But, as at Sinai, salvation is not the point. Stop there, and you slide back into slavery. Deliverance is but the beginning of God's process.

"If I be lifted up," said this God of Mount Calvary, *"I will draw all men to myself."*[214]

Another time, He *"went up on a mountainside and called to him those he wanted, and they came to him."*[215]

Wherever He calls you *from*, God brings you *to* Mount Calvary to meet Him. Deliverance must lead to the divine encounter.

And when you meet God, you will be transformed.

"To all who received him, who believed in his name, he gave the power to become," not the children of Israel, but *"the children of God"* Himself.[216]

And still God is adding citizens to that holy nation set apart to serve Him.[217] Only now, the transformation is taking place at Calvary, God's *new* holy mountain.

"You shall receive power," He says, *"...and be my witnesses... to the end of the earth."*[218]

And the law given to form the holy nation God has called out of bondage and into His service?

---

[212] 1 Corinthians 15:26, 54-56.
[213] Hebrews 10:12.
[214] John 12:32, KJV.
[215] Mark 3:13, NIV.
[216] John 1:12, NIV.
[217] 1 Peter 2:9.
[218] Acts 1:8, NIV.

A new commandment: *"Love one another as I have loved you. By this shall all men know that you are my disciples—that you love one another."*[219] By this shall all men know Who the God of Calvary—and Sinai—is.

இ⊶ளு

Why have you been saved—assuming you've come out of the bondage to sin from which God has freed you?

You have been saved—brought out—to meet God. The change God has made in your life is intended to lead to a change in your relationship with God—to create a relationship of love with God where none existed before (on your part, anyway).

And *what* is supposed to come out of this encounter with God besides a new relationship?

A transformed life for you.

Whatever your life has been—whatever *you* have been—God invites you to let Him turn you into His ambassador to the world—a mediator of His grace to others—a citizen of His chosen and set-apart people—a partner in fulfilling His purpose for all Creation.

And *how* are you to be this special spiritual agent of God?

By living your life according to His law—His gracious gift for knowing how to obey Him. You do not get salvation by obeying any law. Instead, by obeying God's law, you get the privilege of offering salvation to others—and the possibility of bringing others to the mountain where God is—where God waits to meet them and transform them—in the place where heaven will touch earth again.

இ⊶ளு

---

[219] John 13:34-35, NIV.

From the Book of Numbers

Numbers 32:20-23 RSV

[20] So Moses said to them, "If you will do this, if you will take up arms to go before the Lord for the war, [21] and every armed man of you will pass over the Jordan before the Lord, until he has driven out his enemies from before him [22] and the land is subdued before the Lord; then after that you shall return and be free of obligation to the Lord and to Israel; and this land shall be your possession before the Lord. [23] But if you will not do so, behold, you have sinned against the Lord; and be sure your sin will find you out."

ॐॳॳ

22.

Be Sure Your Sin Will Find You Out

Numbers 32:20-23 RSV

A friend of mine has been in the news of late. I met him several years ago when we were both working in the Navy Annex in Washington. He would come down where the chaplains were, from time to time, to "shoot the breeze" for a while.

My friend was an interesting fellow. He was a Navy captain, with an important job in Marine Corps Headquarters. He had been an Army medic in Viet Nam. He had earned a doctorate in pharmacy and he was later ordained as an Episcopal priest. He had more ribbons on his uniform than anybody I had ever seen in person.

Earlier this month, I opened the local paper to find my friend's picture on the front page. It turns out that many of the medals he wore all those years he did not "rate." He was court-marshaled and is now in jail, revealed to the world as a fraud. After 34 years in the military, his secret dishonor caught up with him.

It's just like that ominous warning buried deep in the pages of the Old Testament: *"Be sure your sin will find you out."*

కొుడ్

Now, preachers are taught to deal with biblical passages in context. In this case, the context is Moses leading the 12 tribes of Israel into the Promised Land and demanding that all of them share the full risk of military conquest. The story is told in Numbers, Chapter 32.

Moses tells some of the tribes that if they do not go and fight alongside the others as they have promised, they will have sinned against God.

And then Moses warns them: *"Be sure your sin will find you out."* They don't argue the point with him. They know he's right. They've seen it happen too many times before to have any doubts.

But this morning, I want to take this portion of a verse completely out of its context. I want to pull this warning right out of the story in Numbers because it has a universal application. I want to take this verse out of its historical context so that I can put it in your *personal* context—and mine.

As Moses said to them over three thousand years ago, so I say to you today: *"Be sure your sin will find you out."*

❧

It's a sobering thought. But is it true? Will your sin really "find you out"? How do you know?

Well, the Bible says it will, and *that* should be proof enough. And the Bible gives some pretty impressive examples: In Genesis, Cain lures his brother Abel out into a field, away from any people, and kills him. There are no witnesses, but God confronts Cain, saying, *"…the blood of your brother is crying to me from the ground. And now you are cursed…."*[220]

Jonah tries to run away from the assignment God gives him and the Bible says, *"…the Lord hurled a great wind upon the sea, and there was a mighty tempest on the sea, so that the ship threatened to break*

---

[220] Genesis 4:10-11, RSV.

up…. And the Lord appointed a great fish to swallow up Jonah; and Jonah was in the belly of the fish three days and three nights."[221]

In the New Testament, in the Book of Acts, Ananias and Sapphira sell their property and donate *part* of the money to the Jerusalem church, pretending they're giving *all* of it, and Peter says to Sapphira, *"How is it that you have agreed together to tempt the Spirit of the Lord? The feet of those that have buried your husband are at the door and they will carry you out."*[222]

కిళ్ళ

The Bible says, *"your sin will find you out."* But many people don't accept the authority of the Bible these days. Many people today obviously doubt that the warning is true. Some, if their behavior is any indication, are convinced that it *isn't* true. But there are countless contemporary examples. They're in the paper every day.

Will your sin find you out?

Count on it.

Sometimes, there will be enemies who will do all they can to bring your sins to light, assuming that doing so will give them the upper hand. There are even people who will dig for the dirt on you when there's nothing in it for them—except the chance to hurt you.

కిళ్ళ

But don't blame it on the people who expose your sin—it's your sin that will have found you out. And it doesn't require the involvement of someone intentionally working against you.

You see, the very consequences of your sin can bring your sin to light. Sin sets in motion a series of events that may soon run well beyond your control: a chain reaction of causes and effects. You can try to hide your sin, but the effort to hide a sin often requires additional sin—greater sin—to keep it all under wraps.

---

[221] Jonah 1:4, 17, RSV.
[222] Acts 5:9, RSV.

But the lies and schemes can't hide a sin forever. They just add to the magnitude of it when it finally does come to light. Cover-ups never cover everything. And all cover-ups are temporary. You may sin in secret, but there is no "secret sin."

Your sin will find you out. You can run from your sin, but you cannot hide from it—not forever. And it doesn't matter whether you think you are sinning for a good reason or for a bad reason, it's still sin. The reason is only good or bad as *you* define it. If the reason were good by God's definition, then it wouldn't be sin in the first place.

If you sin, just expect that accountability is coming. You have to deal with sin—in this world or in the next.

❦

Your sin will find you out because sin is not benign. It is always malignant. It grows. It metastasizes. It mutates. It is intent on revealing itself in some sick way. And it does not care what impact it has on you. When you give in to the allure of sin, you give sin power over you. And sin will use that power against you, and against people and things you care about. The purpose—the mission—of sin is to destroy—to eat away at anything good like acid. Paul says, *"The wages of sin is death."*[223]

This may sound like bad news. It is also good news. Let me explain: *"Be sure your sin will find you out"* means that there will be an automatic, non-overcome-able consequence that your sin sets in motion. In most people, the damage that comes with this process slows down the destructive momentum of sin.

"The wages of sin is death," but before you get there and experience eternal damnation, you generally get to results like shame and sickness, broken marriages, complicated lives and financial loss. Your sin has found you out along the way and you're

---

[223] Romans 3:23, RSV.

just not as eager to follow it anymore like the giddy, gullible fool you were when you went along with it before.

Are there sins you wish you hadn't committed? Are there sins that blew up in your face—even years later? Are there sins you thought you had completely and permanently hidden that came back like a ghost from the grave to destroy dreams and hopes, relationships and reputations, health and peace?

It could be worse—and will be—if something doesn't happen.

Unfortunately, most people don't turn away from sin until it finally finds them out.

On the other hand, fortunately, a lot of people do finally turn away from sin because it has finally found them out often enough. They just don't want to wake up with any more hangovers or unexpected tattoos. They don't want to pay any more fines or try to come up with a new batch of excuses. They finally decide they don't want to destroy their health, or their hopes, or their families.

Believing that your sin will find you out is a way of taking what's happened to you already—the sin that's already found you out—and projecting that experience across the rest of your life: "If *that* sin found me out, my other sins probably will, too—given time. And since I hated it when that sin found me out, I'll probably hate it just as much or more when any other sins I commit find me out, so maybe I ought to just drop them now and spare myself the misery."

∞

Sin is just not worth it.

"Be sure your sin will find you out," the Bible says. Do not be in doubt about this fact. Just know it's going to be this way. It's a "given." Don't try to beat the system. Count the cost ahead of time[224] and act according to your long-term best interest.

Why will your sins find you out?

---

[224] Luke 14:28.

C. S. Lewis explains it this way: People think some things are right and some things are wrong, and we try to convince others that we are right. By doing this, we act as though we are right, or they are wrong, as compared to an independent standard. We may disagree as to what right and wrong are at this point or that, but the fact that we talk about right and wrong at all supports the idea of the standard—and of something behind it all.

Lewis suggests that the "something" is like a mind—conscious, purposeful and preferring one thing to another. Somebody or something, he says, wants us to behave a certain way. There is a system of right and wrong in reality, and a Power that sustains the system.[225]

In the baseball movie *Bull Durham*,[226] there is a wise and experienced catcher who is teaching an inexperienced and foolish pitcher to submit to the catcher's will and throw the pitches the catcher calls for. The pitcher wants to call his own pitches and rejects the catcher's signals. So the catcher lets the pitcher throw what he wants to throw.

But the catcher also tells the batter what pitch is coming, and the batter hits it out of the park. The catcher's message to the pitcher is, "I call the shots. Throw what I tell you to throw. If you don't, be sure your sin will find you out—because I will see to it."

Your sin will find you out because God wants it to—and will ensure that it does—if not right away, then in time, when the consequences may be even worse. Don't bet against a righteous God. The odds are not in your favor. No one "gets away with it," not as long as God awaits us at the final judgment[227] and, as Paul puts it in Romans 2, *"their conflicting thoughts accuse ... them on that day when...God judges the secrets of men by Christ Jesus."*[228]

---

[225] C. S. Lewis, "The Law of Human Nature," from *Mere Christianity*, 1943.
[226] Movie *Bull Durham*, 1988.
[227] Revelation 20:11-15.
[228] Romans 2:15-16, RSV.

"Be sure your sin will find you out."

If true, what's the point?

Don't sin. Just don't do it!

If you have sinned, cut your losses. Stop doing it—right now. Make confession to God and retribution to any victims where you can do so without inflicting more pain.

God doesn't condone sin. He doesn't ignore it or accept it. There is no place you can hide from your sin—except in Jesus. God doesn't condone sin, but He will forgive it, through and for Jesus.

Paul presents the options in Romans, Chapter 6: *"...what return did you get from the things of which you are now ashamed? The end of those things is death. But now that you have been set free from sin and have become slaves of God, the return you get is sanctification and its end, eternal life. For the wages of sin is death, but the free gift of God is eternal life in Christ Jesus our Lord."*[229]

❧

---

[229] Romans 6:21-23, RSV.

From the Book of Deuteronomy

Deuteronomy 8:7-18 RSV

[Moses said:]

[7] "...the LORD your God is bringing you into a good land, a land of brooks of water, of fountains and springs, flowing forth in valleys and hills, [8] a land of wheat and barley, of vines and fig trees and pomegranates, a land of olive trees and honey, [9] a land in which you will eat bread without scarcity, in which you will lack nothing, a land whose stones are iron, and out of whose hills you can dig copper. [10] And you shall eat and be full, and you shall bless the LORD your God for the good land he has given you.

[11] "Take heed lest you forget the LORD your God, by not keeping his commandments and his ordinances and his statutes, which I command you this day: [12] lest, when you have eaten and are full, and have built goodly houses and live in them, [13] and when your herds and flocks multiply, and your silver and gold is multiplied, and all that you have is multiplied, [14] then your heart be lifted up, and you forget the LORD your God, who brought you out of the land of Egypt, out of the house of bondage, [15] who led you through the great and terrible wilderness, with its fiery serpents and scorpions and thirsty ground where there was no water, who brought you water out of the flinty rock, [16] who fed you in the wilderness with manna which your fathers did not know, that he might humble you and test you, to do you good in the end. [17] Beware lest you say in your heart, 'My power and the might of my hand have gotten me this wealth.' [18] You shall remember the LORD your God, for it is he who gives you power to get wealth; that he may confirm his covenant which he swore to your fathers, as at this day."

৯৽৶

23.

Lest We Forget

Deuteronomy 8:7-18 RSV

If you went over to the new Family Service Center behind the Exchange on base,[230] and told the young lady at the reception desk you were being transferred far away, she would show you a DVD of your future home. You would see all the good things about where you're going, and you would hear some very good advice about how to adapt and thrive in the new location. Family Service Centers provide these resources so that you can have a positive experience and fulfill your purpose in going to your new home.

In the eighth chapter of Deuteronomy, the children of Israel were about to complete a homeport change that had been in progress for 40 years. And their commanding officer wanted to make sure they appreciated what a great duty station they were going to. He wanted to make sure they were properly grateful to their Detailer for "cutting" these particular orders for them.

This was a dream assignment, but if they didn't meet the minimum performance requirements, this Detailer could "short tour" them in a heartbeat. There were plenty of arduous duty

---

[230] This is another sermon preached in a Navy Chapel (and before the Internet hit its stride).

stations for those who didn't appreciate blessings when they had them.

So let's summarize: Appreciate what you have, and respect the One Who gave it to you.

As a Navy chaplain, I stood at the Berlin Wall many years ago, before it was torn down, taking pictures of armed communist guards prepared to gun down anyone trying to get *out* of *their* country. Some of you have been to Gitmo or Haiti or the Mexican border where boatloads and truckloads of people risk their lives trying to get *into our* country.

Those who would die for what we have remind us that what we have is *"a good land...a land in which you...eat bread without scarcity, in which you...lack for nothing...."* We are, of all people on earth, most fortunate. Ours is a great land.

But *we* did not make it so.

America's beauty and its abundance were well in place when our ancestors arrived—*whenever* they arrived. The wise among them recognized this divine gift and responded accordingly: They celebrated their great good fortune by giving thanks to God and encouraging their children to continue the practice.

Today,[231] we celebrate the miracle our ancestors discovered, the miracle we continue to discover when we open our eyes to the splendor and majesty, the bounty and benevolence, of the place and experience we call "America." We celebrate the totally unnecessary fact that we live *here*, and not somewhere else on this globe. We celebrate the equally unnecessary fact that *we* live here, and not somebody else. Us.

❧◦❧

But along with the miracle we celebrate, there is a mystery we acknowledge. What we do with the land we possess, and how we relate to the One Who gave it to us, determine how long we will

---

[231] Thanksgiving Day.

be allowed to enjoy this good land, and how much joy it will bring us.

Just as God established a covenant with His people through Moses so they could live in harmony with neighbors and in humble obedience before God, so Pilgrims, Puritans, and even profiteers in this country made solemn commitments to order their personal lives and their social organizations in ways that glorified God's gift and submitted to His will. They were insufficiently modern and sophisticated to suppose that there was no link between the morality of their behavior and the well-being of their society.

They did not realize that it was hopelessly naive to think there was a loving, generous God who chose, for no reason other than His own unfathomable purpose, to place these particular people in this particular land, or that He cared about how they treated the land—and Him—while they enjoyed the blessings of peace and prosperity He had given them.

Moses, the man who led the Hebrew people from nothingness to nationhood, was convinced of the need to revere and obey God. George Washington, the man who more than anyone else turned the American rabble into a republic, expressed very similar sentiments:

> "...I do recommend and assign Thursday,
> the 26th of November next,
> to be devoted by the people of the [United] States
> to the service of that great and glorious Being
> Who is the beneficent Author of all the good
> that was, that is, and that will be,
> that we may then unite in rendering unto Him
> our sincere and humble thanks...
> for all the great and various favors
> which He has been pleased to confer upon us."[232]

❧

---

[232] George Washington, *Presidential Thanksgiving Proclamation*, October 3, 1789.

As we worship—as we celebrate our unbelievably good fortune—let us also remember. Let us remember that:

> "...grace has brought us safe thus far,
> and grace will lead us home."[233]

Let us remember that God not only gives us wonderful gifts, He also gives us a trustworthy instruction guide to ensure proper use of what we have. Let us remember that God gives so that He can enjoy us while *we* enjoy the gifts He has given us, all in a holy and righteous relationship with Him.

Whereas the liturgy of these people assembled before Moses should have been, "I just can't thank God enough," they were instead a people who grew frustrated in the face of adversity and arrogant in the arms of good fortune.

But don't get smug, for the same temptation stalks *us*, on this day, in this nation, as part of this generation.

Today, let us trade frustration for faith and arrogance for appreciation.

Let us fill our hearts with love for this land and loyalty to the One Who bestowed it so freely upon us.

Let us remember what God has done for us, and what God requires of us.

Let us remember, on *this* day of all days.

Let us remember, lest we forget.

৵৽৵

---

[233] From John Newton, "Amazing Grace," 1779.

Deuteronomy 26:1-11 NRSV

[Moses said:]

¹ *When you have come into the land that the Lord your God is giving you as an inheritance to possess, and you possess it, and settle in it,* ² *you shall take some of the first of all the fruit of the ground, which you harvest from the land that the Lord your God is giving you, and you shall put it in a basket and go to the place that the Lord your God will choose as a dwelling for his name.* ³ *You shall go to the priest who is in office at that time, and say to him, " Today I declare to the Lord your God that I have come into the land that the Lord swore to our ancestors to give us."* ⁴ *When the priest takes the basket from your hand and sets it down before the altar of the Lord your God,* ⁵ *you shall make this response before the Lord your God: "A wandering Aramean was my ancestor; he went down into Egypt and lived there as an alien, few in number, and there he became a great nation, mighty and populous.* ⁶ *When the Egyptians treated us harshly and afflicted us, by imposing hard labor on us,* ⁷ *we cried to the Lord, the God of our ancestors; the Lord heard our voice and saw our affliction, our toil, and our oppression.* ⁸ *The Lord brought us out of Egypt with a mighty hand and an outstretched arm, with a terrifying display of power, and with signs and wonders;* ⁹ *and he brought us into this place and gave us this land, a land flowing with milk and honey.* ¹⁰ *So now I bring the first of the fruit of the ground that you, O Lord, have given me." You shall set it down before the Lord your God and bow down before the Lord your God.* ¹¹ *Then you, together with the Levites and the aliens who reside among you, shall celebrate with all the bounty that the Lord your God has given to you and to your house.*

৵৽

24.

The Story of First Fruits

Deuteronomy 26:1-11 NRSV

Here we are again, in the usual place at the appointed time with our familiar liturgy for worship. But suppose we went back for a few minutes this morning to a time and place very much unlike our own. Let's go back thousands of years—to a place thousands of miles away.

The people of this other time and place live in villages much smaller and more primitive than ours.[234] They farm little patches of ground and tend a few olive and fig trees. From our perspective, their lives seem hard, dull and precarious.

But, as it turns out, they see their lives in a very different light. You get a sense of this when they gather up the first fruits of their harvests and take them to their holy sites and set them down before their God. Listen to what they say:

"Today, I declare to the Lord God that I have come into the land that the Lord swore to our ancestors to give us."

৵৵

---

[234] This sermon was preached in the village of Pinehurst, North Carolina.

Each person affirms in the presence of God that he or she has received *personally* what God promised a particular *family* that extends through many generations. The land that produced the crops these people brought—the land upon which they make their homes—belongs to God and has been given to them by God as an undeserved gift.

These people know some things in their basic existence that we in our sophisticated version no longer do: Land is food—and food is life. And they know that God gave them their land. Therefore, God gave them their food. Therefore, God gave them, and continues to give them, life.

In their simple, homemade baskets, they take what the ground has given and go to worship the God Who gave them ground and goods alike as a gift. And they repeat as their call to worship a story as familiar to them as this morning's liturgy is to you. It begins: *"A wandering Aramean was my father,"* and goes on to remember a time when this family had no land, no freedom, no peace and, seemingly, no hope.

With the first fruits of their fields lying at their feet, the farmers then proclaim to themselves and everyone around them—and to God—that God brought their ancestors (and therefore them) out of bondage and want. They testify publicly that God brought their ancestors (and therefore them) into a land that produces food and sustains life. Everything they now have in life, including life itself, is a gift from God, and they would not have it if He had not chosen to give it.

Working a land of milk and honey is not a hard life when you remember there was a time when your family had no land at all. Living the life of a subsistence farmer is not precarious when you know that your ancestors lived their lives as slaves. The daily routine of life on the land is not dull when you know that you live each day in covenant relationship with the God Who created heaven and earth and controls past, present and future.

☙◦❧

So they retell the story that puts their lives in proper perspective and conclude by saying, *"So now I bring the first of the fruit of the ground that you, O Lord, have given me."* And they give their offering, setting it down before the Lord. And they bow down in worship before the Lord. And then they celebrate all the bounty that the Lord has given them. They celebrate along with all the others who will benefit, as God intends, from what each person brings.

A primitive time and place…but the truth is the same, timeless and universal:

> "We give [God] but [His] own,
> whate'er the gift may be.
> All that we have is [His] alone,
> A trust, O Lord, from Thee."[235]

❧❧

A wandering Armenian was your father (spiritually). A crucified Galilean, his Descendent, is your Savior. All that you have is a gift from the God Who blessed the one and raised the Other.

Celebrate what God has given you by giving Him what He requires.

❧❧

---

[235] William Walsham How, "We Give Thee But Thine Own," 1858.

From the Book of Joshua

25.

Memorial Stones

Joshua 3 and 4 RSV

Before coming to Little Creek[236] last summer, I worked in the Washington, D.C., area, in a building called the Navy Annex,[237] which overlooks the Pentagon. Across the street from both the Navy Annex and the Pentagon is Arlington National Cemetery. Every day, from our building, we could see funerals taking place in Arlington. We watched as some of the "9/11" victims were buried there, and later, casualties from the Afghanistan and Iraqi war zones.

Serenity reigns at Arlington, disturbed only by the rifle volleys of honor guards paying a nation's final tribute to service men and women as they are laid to rest. And this weekend, soldiers of the Army's "Old Guard" have placed a flag on every grave, in recognition of the sacrifices made by those who sleep beneath the simple stones.

Beneath each stone: a life given. Behind each life: a story whose briefest summary is carved into the stone. *Each* stone is a memorial,

---

[236] Now known as Joint Expeditionary Base Little Creek-Fort Story, in Hampton Roads, Virginia.
[237] The "Annex" has since been demolished and the land made part of an expanded Arlington Cemetery.

but *together* they form an enduring monument —perhaps the most powerful monument of all—to what America stands for and what Americans prize.

Tomorrow,[238] our President will go to Arlington and stand before one very special stone. On that great stone are inscribed the words: "Known Only to God."

The highest leader of our government will decorate that stone with flowers and extol the sacrifice of all those who have given their lives in the defense of this country.

But the truth is that only God knows, not just the identity of unknown soldiers, but the sacrifices made, and the burdens carried, in *every* human life.

And so, as this weekend invites us to look again at our memorials, and remember what they mean, let me invite your attention to another monument, another grouping of memorial stones. These stones are from the Jordan River, and the monument is to God.

The story is simple: God led the children of Israel out of a desert wilderness and into the Promised Land of Canaan. To get them from one to the other, He brought them across the Jordan River. God brought them across a Jordan that dried up when they stepped into it—and flowed again only when they all had crossed safely over to the other side. Crossing over the Jordan on dry ground was a miracle that became a memorial.

The story is told in the Old Testament, in the 3rd and 4th chapters of the Book of Joshua. Time and clarity argue against reading *all* of both chapters. If you will permit me—trust me—to draw out for you the central story, I will read you an abridged version. I promise to leave out nothing essential—and to *add* nothing at all.

---

[238] Memorial Day.

From Joshua 3:

¹ Early in the morning Joshua and all the Israelites…went to the Jordan, where they camped before crossing over. ² After three days, the officers went throughout the camp, giving orders to the people, "When you see the ark of the covenant of the LORD your God…follow it. ⁴ Then you will know which way to go, since you have never been this way before.…"

⁵ Joshua told the people, "Consecrate yourselves, for tomorrow the LORD will do amazing things among you."

⁹ Joshua said to the Israelites, "Come here and listen to the words of the LORD your God. ¹⁰ This is how you will know that the living God is among you.… ¹¹ See, the ark of the covenant of the Lord of all the earth will go into the Jordan ahead of you. ¹²…its waters flowing downstream will be cut off and stand up in a heap."

¹⁶ …so the people crossed over .…

And from Chapter 4:

¹ …the LORD said to Joshua, ² "…tell them to take up twelve stones from the middle of the Jordan…and to carry them over with you and put them down at the place where you stay tonight.

⁶ "These stones are to be a memorial to the people of Israel forever."

⁸ So the Israelites did as Joshua commanded them. They took twelve stones from the middle of the Jordan…and they carried them over with them to their camp, where they put them down.

²⁰ And Joshua set up…the twelve stones they had taken out of the Jordan. ²¹ He said to the Israelites, "In the future when your descendants ask their fathers, 'What do these stones mean?' ²² tell them, 'Israel crossed the Jordan on dry ground.' ²³ For the LORD your God dried up the Jordan before you until you had crossed over.…

²⁴ "He did this so that all the peoples of the earth might know that the hand of the LORD is powerful and so that you might always fear the LORD your God."

৵৵

The miracle became a memorial that day—and then later, it became a metaphor. For centuries, "crossing over the Jordan"[239] has been a metaphor for the death experience of a Christian. When the children of Israel crossed over the Jordan, they left behind a lifetime of wandering in the wilderness—and inherited a new life of joy in the Promised Land.

The Christian church came to see the physical life as a season of wandering in this world that "the redeemed of the Lord" would gladly leave behind[240] when it came time to enter "the land that is fairer than day."[241]

The difference between life and death has been marked in many cultures by the image of a dividing river,[242] but for the Christian, it is one special river, the Jordan River, whose waters were parted by God when it was time for the child of God to come home.

∾

Today, I would like to offer you this image of "crossing over Jordan" as a metaphor, not for death, but for life. As we journey through our lives, could we not say that the process for each of us is like crossing over our own personal "Jordans"?

You pass through your life, from one side to the other, surrounded by all the others who are "crossing over" with you— some ahead, some behind, others alongside. As the scripture says, *"All the people were crossing the Jordan,"* but each one of them experienced it uniquely, as a personal event.

Day by day, year after year, you live your life—you make your pilgrimage through this world—you cross your Jordan. It is the great human passage.

---

[239] See, for example, William Williams, "Guide Me, O Thou Great Jehovah," verse 3, 1745; Translator, Peter Williams, 1771.
[240] 2 Corinthians 5:8.
[241] From Sanford Fillmore Bennett, "In the Sweet By and By," verse 1, 1868.
[242] See, for example, the theme of the dead crossing the River Styx to the underworld in classic Greek mythology.

Today, some of you are just beginning, while others of you suppose you're nearly done. A few of us will be surprised when we find "the far shore" turns out to be much closer than it looked, and all of us will probably wonder (when we get to the other side) how we ever got there so fast.

So if this experience we call "life" is in some way a Jordan-like crossing, what can we learn as we come once more to these memorial stones in Joshua and consider the miracle they recall?

৯০৶

The first lesson to learn about crossing your Jordan is surprisingly simple. The Israelites were told: *"When you see the ark of the covenant...follow it."*

The ark of the covenant was the symbol of the presence of God with His people. It was the earthly throne of the heavenly King. The ark is gone now, but the God Whose presence it symbolized is very real, and He is just as involved in the lives of His children today as He was then.

God is bringing us through our Jordans just like He brought them. The signs of His presence are all around us. If you look for Him, you will find Him—and when you see God, you should follow.

"When you see...the Lord your God, you are to...follow...then you will know which way to go, since" (as the Bible says) *"you have never been this way before."*

That's why we sing, "Guide me, O Thou Great Jehovah"[243] and "Lead on, O King Eternal."[244] None of us knows enough from personal experience to cross the Jordan successfully without God's help. We don't know which way to go in this life. Contrary to the assurances of the "reincarnation crowd," we have never been this way before.

243 William Williams, "Guide Me, O Thou Great Jehovah," verse 3, 1745; Translator, Peter Williams, 1771.
244 Ernest W. Shurtleff, "Lead on, O King Eternal," 1887.

Why would anybody with any sense expect to know how or where to cross his or her Jordan?

You do need someone to lead and guide you—Someone like the great and eternal King, Jehovah.

It's a whole lot easier to cross your Jordan—to live your life—on solid ground, the way God's children did, than to fight the raging waters of this life in your own strength alone. Many who try are swept along to their eventual doom by powerful and deceptive currents they do not foresee and cannot control.

But if you choose to cross your Jordan by following where God leads you, you will cross where He has already parted the waters. He will see you safely through to the other side.

❧

Now, you would think that everyone would want to line up behind a God Who parts the waters and puts a solid foundation beneath you. But look around and you will see that people are constantly and compulsively hunting for their own way to cross the Jordan.

The reason is that crossing the Jordan with God—even on the solid ground He always provides those who cross with Him—is no cakewalk. You have to *consecrate* yourself.

(And here, we take a time out to define our terms.)

To "consecrate" means to set apart for special use. But it's kind of like a telescope: You can look at this consecration business from two different directions. The end you look at makes all the difference in what you see.

When *God* consecrates us as part of our salvation in Jesus Christ, He sets us apart from our sin so that we may be like Christ and come redeemed, cleansed, holy and perfect into His presence. That's when *God* consecrates *us*.

When *we* consecrate *ourselves*, we take a look at everything in our lives and discard the stuff that competes with God for our attention, or blurs our clear vision of God, or simply offends God.

Consecrating ourselves doesn't mean we save ourselves or make ourselves perfect, but it does mean we try to line up squarely behind God for the march across the river.

Paul said to the Romans: *"…present your bodies as a living sacrifice, holy and acceptable to God…."*[245]

The writer of Hebrews said: *"…let us throw off everything that hinders and the sin that so easily entangles, and let us run with perseverance the race marked out for us."*[246]

Joshua said, *"Consecrate yourselves…."*

To consecrate yourself means to accept God's purpose for your life and the meaning He assigns to what happens in it. It means letting God determine where your life is going and how you're going to get there. A lot of people don't want to consecrate themselves to cross their Jordan because it means giving up control over their lives.

You want to control your own life?

You just bought yourself a life that will sooner or later fly out of control.

If you want to cross your Jordan on solid ground, you must give your life over to the control of God Who alone can bring you safely to the other side. Consecrate yourself…and not only will you cross the Jordan, you will see *"the Lord do amazing things among you."* Consecrate yourself…and see.

☜⋅☞

"But what about all my problems?"

"What about my health problems? I live with pain every day," or "The doctor found something…."

"What about my financial problems? I'm not sure my job is going to be here next year," or "We can't seem to make ends meet."

---

245 Romans 12:1, RSV.
246 Hebrews 12:1, RSV.

"What about my family problems? My parents are getting old and will be needing a lot of care," and "There's friction in my marriage," and "My kids—I can't figure them out."

"I'm following the Lord and I've tried to live right, but I've got so much on me right now… How can you call this, 'crossing the Jordan the *easy* way'?"

It's a fair question. When you consecrate yourself, you are (as the writer of Hebrews suggests) getting rid of the *stumbling blocks* in the course you are walking (or running) with God. And when you have done that, and you start across the Jordan, God says, *"Now take stones from here out of the midst of the Jordan, and carry them with you…."*

The burdens you carry now—as you live your life—as you cross the Jordan with God—these are the *building blocks* for a monument—the memorial stones to the miracle of God bringing you safely through this life on solid ground. The burdens you shoulder as you cross the Jordan are a witness to the world, and a sacred reminder to you, that God was and is and always will be present and powerful enough to sustain you in the crossing you have to make but cannot survive without His saving grace. The greater the stones you carry through the Jordan, whether by choice or by chance, the greater the monument will be when you lay these burdens down on the other side.

೩–೨

What do I mean by "building locks"?

Two things: The stones you carry through life "by choice" are those sacrificial commitments you make to consecrate yourself to God—those things that "cost" you in some way. The stones of "choice" are those things you do—or refuse to do—that set you apart from the common culture around you, and may set you up for the distrust, ridicule, rejection or hostility of others.

I'm talking about things like regular prayer, worship and scripture study, wholesome speech and moral habits, sexual abstinence before, and fidelity during, marriage, financial stewardship and sacrificial service, in the church and out.

The stones you carry "by chance" are those burdens and afflictions you would not have chosen, but which are thrust upon you unbidden in the normal course of life.

Of course, by embracing the consecrated life, and the "choice" stones that go with it, you will certainly avoid many of the "chance" stones that naturally accumulate in the unconsecrated life. Many, but not all.

It is not in the nature of the Jordan crossing that, even when God parts the water, all the stones will be washed away. No, you will encounter some "chance" stones. They include all sorts of pain and sorrow: illnesses and injuries, conflicts and temptations, disappointments and dangers, losses and grief.

These "chance stones" become *memorial* stones by the way you carry them—with courage and faith and dependence on God—by bearing their weight in your life so that they become the focus of God's redeeming and refining activity in you as you make your way with Him across the Jordan.

No one wants to carry the "chance" stones of life, but somehow carrying the "choice" stones as well makes it easier rather than harder to carry the "chance" stones placed upon you. And all are easier to carry on the solid footing God provides. Together, what you carry—and how you carry it—in the end create the monument that is the message and tribute of your life.

છ્ન્ઝ

And what is the point of this monument your sacrifices and your struggles and your sufferings erect?

Well, what's the point of dying for your country?

Some might say that the answer to that question is, "...to secure the Blessings of Liberty to ourselves and our posterity."[247]

---

[247] From the Preamble to the U.S. Constitution, 1787.

Joshua told the children of Israel, crossing the Jordan on solid ground, burdened but joyful, "The monument you erect with the stones you carry will be the thing you point your children to, to light the way for your posterity, physical *and spiritual*, so that they, too, may enjoy the blessings of a liberating journey with God as *they* make *their* way across *their* Jordan."

"You shall let your children know that '…the Lord your God dried up the waters of the Jordan for you until you passed over.…'"

And surviving your struggles, your sacrifices, and your suffering by consecrating yourself and following your God, step by step, into and through the Jordan, is how that sign—that monument to God's power in your life—gets built.

According to Abraham Lincoln, thousands of Americans gave their lives around a sleepy Pennsylvania village so that "…this nation, under God, might have a new birth of freedom.…"[248]

It does not seem unreasonable for this God, Who has given us a new *spiritual* birth—and freedom from sin—in His Son Jesus Christ—it does not seem unreasonable for this God to call you and me to give our lives over to His purpose and direction so that *"all the peoples of the world may know that the hand of the Lord is powerful"*—powerful enough to part the waters when they are going under, to save them and bring them safely to Jordan's other side.

⚜

But there is one thing more.

When you consecrate yourself and follow God's leading across the Jordan—when you pick up the stones you encounter in the Jordan and faithfully shoulder those burdens as you journey on across—when you use those stones to erect the memorial to God's miraculous power at work in and for your life—you carve a message in your memory that protects you, lest you forget. The

---

[248] From *The Gettysburg Address*, Abraham Lincoln, November 19, 1863.

suffering and sacrifice of the life consecrated and committed to God ensures that you do not forget to fear God.

(Again, time out to define a term.)

"The fear of the Lord is the beginning of wisdom."[249]

It is not to be terrified, as one *might* be at the prospect of spending eternity cut off from God's presence, and as one *should* be at the prospect of trying to cross over life's Jordan River apart from God's power.

"The fear of the Lord" is awe and respect—a proper appreciation for what He has done, and will yet do, to get you across your Jordan. *"The fear of the Lord"* is an unwavering concentration on your assigned position in relation to God in the great, lifelong march "across the river."

If you fear God, you do not have to fear the Jordan—or the idea of crossing it. To fear God is to live fearlessly, knowing you are going across in the care of One Who parts the waters for you and sets your feet on solid ground.

How is your journey across the Jordan going? Are you drowning in currents you can't control, weighed down by burdens you cannot carry alone?

Or are you crossing your Jordan on dry ground—solid ground—on Christ the Solid Rock?[250]

What message will the monument of your life convey, when you get to the other side?

❧

---

[249] Proverbs 9:10, RSV.

[250] See Edward Mote, "My Hope is Built on Nothing Less," (refrain), 1834.

Joshua 24:1, 14-18 ESV

¹ *Joshua gathered all the tribes of Israel to Shechem and summoned the elders, the heads, the judges, and the officers of Israel. And they presented themselves before God.*

¹⁴ *"Now therefore fear the LORD and serve him in sincerity and in faithfulness. Put away the gods that your fathers served beyond the River and in Egypt, and serve the LORD.* ¹⁵ *And if it is evil in your eyes to serve the LORD, choose this day whom you will serve, whether the gods your fathers served in the region beyond the River, or the gods of the Amorites in whose land you dwell. But as for me and my house, we will serve the LORD."*

¹⁶ *Then the people answered, "Far be it from us that we should forsake the LORD to serve other gods,* ¹⁷ *for it is the LORD our God who brought us and our fathers up from the land of Egypt, out of the house of slavery, and who did those great signs in our sight and preserved us in all the way that we went, and among all the peoples through whom we passed.* ¹⁸ *And the LORD drove out before us all the peoples, the Amorites who lived in the land. Therefore we also will serve the LORD, for he is our God."*

✤

26.

Serving the God You Choose

Joshua 24:1, 14-18 ESV

It is an awesome spectacle: All the tribes of Israel have come to Shechem. Shechem is holy ground. It was the first place Abraham stopped when he came to this land God had promised him hundreds of years before.[251] Abraham set up an altar at Shechem and worshipped God.

Jacob dug a well at Shechem[252] and bought property in the town and built an altar himself.[253] Joseph's bones were brought back from Egypt during the Exodus and finally buried at Shechem.[254] There is sacred history in this place.

Shechem is nestled in a mountain pass in the middle of the Holy Land, and three great roads converge here.[255] Joshua has called all Israel to this sacred site. It is an invitation no one declines. The tribes came down these roads just as they did years before when they were fighting—under Joshua's leadership— for the land God had given them.

---

[251] Genesis 12 6.
[252] John 4:12.
[253] Genesis 33:18-19.
[254] Joshua 24:32.
[255] David A Dorsey, "Shechem and the Road Network of Central Samaria," *Bulletin of the American Schools of Oriental Research*, No. 268 (Nov. 1987), pp. 57-70.

Now Joshua is an old man and the conquest of the Promised Land is behind them. But Joshua remains the leader God chose for them and he has one last divine obligation to fulfill before he dies. Joshua calls Israel, as Moses did before him, to choose the God they will serve.

All the tribes of Israel, God's chosen people, have come to Shechem. And from each camp come the leaders of the tribes to gather around the stone altar Joshua erected here years before,[256] and read again the Ten Commandments Joshua carved into the stone,[257] and to speak for themselves and their people as they stand before their God.

Joshua called them, but they are not here to meet him. They have come to this place that has been so full of God for so long, and it is with God they will do business this day.

❧

And you may wonder: Is all this really necessary? Didn't they do this same thing at Mount Sinai, and 40 years later in Moab, just before they crossed the Jordan and entered the land?

The answer to the second question is "yes" and "no." Yes, the children of Israel agreed at Mount Sinai to bind themselves to God by covenant, but all those people are dead—except for the man who called the rest to Shechem.

And, year by year, the composition of Israel changes. People die, and others come of age and bear the moral responsibility of their maturity. And each must speak for himself.

Is it really necessary to renew their covenant with God?

Yes, it is.

They are not the same people, and the circumstances of their lives are not the same. And truth be told, neither they nor their ancestors were ever very good about keeping the covenant with God for very long.

---

[256] Joshua 8:30.
[257] Joshua 8:32.

The best way these folks can keep the covenant is to renew their commitment to it on a regular basis. And Joshua knows the time for renewal has come.

You would think it would be a no-brainer, but when it comes to spiritual commitment, there are always options—not *good* options—but options people are always willing to choose rather than committing to the God Who delivers His people from bondage and provides for their needs and performs great miracles and protects them from danger and prepares a place for them where they can be in loving fellowship with Him.

And so, because we all tend to take a "What have You done for me lately?" attitude with God, Joshua first reviews the history of God's grace and salvation. He does this because what God has done in the past tells you what He's going to do in the future.

"This is what God has done for you—in case it slipped your mind."

ॐ∽ॐ

And then, Joshua lays out the options: You can have this God, or you can have the gods your ancestors served up north "beyond the Euphrates River" before Abraham gave all that up to come with God here.

Or you can hold onto the gods the Egyptians were serving down south for all those years they were holding onto you.

Or you can serve the gods of the people here in Canaan, whose gods—by the way—couldn't keep *your* God from taking this land *from* them and *giving* it to you."

So, who's your God going to be?

And feeling no need to maintain a strict neutrality in the matter, Joshua marks his ballot and holds it up for all to see: "Whatever you do, here's how I'm voting! I'm voting for God! *As for me and my house, we will serve the Lord!*"

Well, Joshua isn't the leader for nothing. *He* knows how to fire up a crowd, whether it's to motivate warriors for battle or to inspire a nation to spiritual commitment. Their old general throws down the gauntlet, and in an instant, the right response roars up in the throats of the tribal elders at the altar—and then gets picked up by the waves of people gathered on the hillsides all around them, until the answer echoes off the mountains like rolling thunder:

"We—will serve—the Lord!
We—will serve—the Lord!
WE—WILL SERVE—THE LORD!"

৯৽৻৶

Joshua ought to feel pretty good. He ought to take up an offering and send them home.

But that's the problem, and he knows it. The people yelling out their loyalty to God on the holy ground of Shechem are going to go home, and when they get there, what will become of their commitment?

Choosing your God is important—choosing the right God, as we saw recently, is the difference between life and death.

But choosing requires serving. That's what choosing means, really. Everyone chooses his or her God or gods. And you will serve the god you choose. You will *do* based on what you *believe*. It's actually pretty easy to take up the God-chant when you're standing on holy ground and everybody around you is caught up in the same spiritual high, feeling the power of God and giving in to the moment.

৯৽৻৶

But then you go home, and the other gods come calling, the gods of your past, the gods of old (and often bad) habits and worthless ways of thinking—the gods of the people around you— people with foreign mindsets and values with foreign gods to support them. You go back to your home—your life in this unholy world of ours—and all the other little gods clamber for you to serve them, instead.

No doubt, Joshua is thinking about those little idols of wood and stone too many of God's people still keep around their houses for good luck and superstitious fear.

Of course, for us, the other gods have taken on different forms. Now, they are the gods of personal comfort and convenience, the gods of immoral thoughts and deeds, served first in secret and then increasingly in public, the gods of material prosperity above all else. Are you harboring any of these around your house, by any chance?

It doesn't matter so much what you say when you're here on holy ground. You can claim the God of Abraham, Isaac and Jacob "from donuts to dismissal," but if you're holding on to any other gods in your life, you'll be serving them, instead.

In fact, serving is choosing. If you're truly choosing God, you must truly serve Him—in sincerity and truth—which means, as Joshua says, get rid of the other gods. Stop choosing them.

And stop serving them. Just say "no" to everything they want you to do.

If we had read further today in Joshua, you would have heard him say something else: *"Put away the foreign gods that are among you— and yield your heart to the Lord."*

The word is actually "incline." *Incline* your heart to the Lord. Don't be straight up about God. Don't be neutral. Incline yourself to God. Lean into Him and away for anything that competes for your allegiance and loyalty to God. And if you are *slightly* inclined to serve God, work on making the inclination greater and greater. The more inclined you are to God, the less inclined you will be— or can be—to other gods. Serve the God you choose.

ཚ⚬ཚ

Oh, and one more thing: Joshua was choosing for himself— *and* for his household. He could not choose for all the tribes of Israel, but he could choose for those family members over whom he had authority. And he did. He could and did decide what God certain people would serve. And he was accountable to God for doing so.

Our children are—or will be—confronted by many more gods who want to be served than we have ever encountered. You who have children must choose for them and direct their service to God until you are no longer responsible to God for doing so.

God help the parents who are not doing all they can to raise their children *"in the nurture and admonition of the Lord"*[258]—to teach their "house" to serve the Lord—except that God will not help them, because they have *not* chosen Him to serve Him. When the days of God's reckoning come, those parents will have chosen to spend their lives and their children's lives serving other gods—and those gods will be all they will have.

ইঞ্চ

Shechem is a holy place. All of the people of God have been called here to renew their commitment to covenant with the God Who brought them here.

But the choice Israel makes at Shechem must be implemented every day wherever they go from Shechem.

Every day you must choose again the God you have promised to serve. Every day you must serve your God to confirm the choice you have made.

Who will you serve?

Who will you choose?

Who will be your God?

ইঞ্চ

---

[258] Ephesians 6:4, KJV.

Indices

Sermon Titles in Alphabetical Order

Text	Title	Page

Sermon Texts in Biblical Order

Sermon Texts in Lectionary Order

Sermon Texts in Lectionary Order

Sermon Texts in Lectionary Order

Related Sermons in Other Volumes

Additional Scripture Passages Referenced

Additional Scripture Passages Referenced

Additional Scripture Passages Referenced

Additional Scripture Passages Referenced

www.ingramcontent.com/pod-product-compliance
Lightning Source LLC
Chambersburg PA
CBHW020849090426
42736CB00008B/295